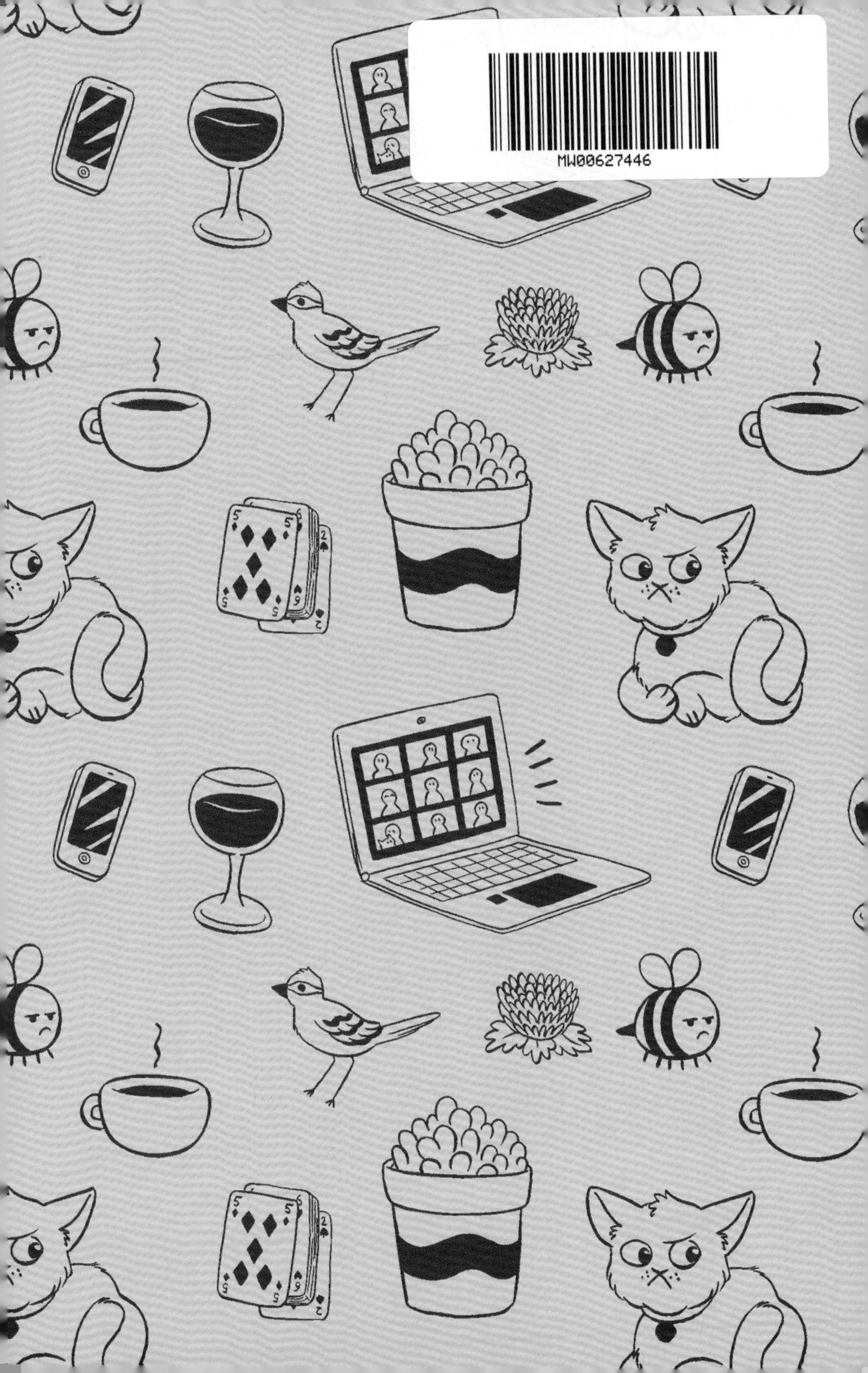

PRAISE FOR RACHAEL SMITH

'Brilliantly observed and illustrated stories of everyday triumphs, failures, and insecurities.'
Adam Buxton

'No wonder people respond strongly to Rachael's work, brave is a term people like to bandy around personal comics, but it's appropriate sometimes. The real wonder of her work is the easy comic touch.'
**Kate Beaton, author of *Hark! A Vagrant*,
King Baby, and *The Princess and the Pony***

'Bloody brilliant storytelling, bloody brilliant comics ... I honestly dare you not to be impressed.'
Richard Bruton, Forbidden Planet International

PRAISE FOR QUARANTINE COMIX

'Rachael Smith's trademark bittersweet, funny and very personal comics make for the perfect chronicle of the weird times we've been living through. They are funny and sad and relatable and wise.'
Chris Addison, comedian and director of *Veep*

'In a period where every day seemed the same, Rachael found a way to make every day different. A tiny, comforting light of understanding, humour and hope in a dark time.'
Kieron Gillen, author and creator of *The Wicked + The Divine*

'One of 2020's most remarkable achievements in comics.'
Broken Frontier

'These comics were a lifeline to so many of us. A ridiculous, humane, insightful, pointed lifeline.'
Paul Cornell, author of *London Falling* and the *Witches of Lynchford* series

'A total joy.'
James Moran, screenwriter, *Severance*

'Harrowing! Heartfelt! Hilarious! Cartoonist Rachael Smith's *Quarantine Comix* are a brutally honest assessment of our internal strife, with more vim and vigour than a Yorkie bar and wine chaser.'
Shelly Bond, creator/editor of Black Crown

'One of the best things to come out of lockdown.'
Lew Stringer, comic artist

Published in the UK and the USA in 2021 by
Icon Books Ltd, Omnibus Business Centre,
39–41 North Road, London N7 9DP
email: info@iconbooks.com
www.iconbooks.com

Sold in the UK, Europe and Asia
by Faber & Faber Ltd, Bloomsbury House,
74–77 Great Russell Street,
London WC1B 3DA or their agents

Distributed in the UK, Europe and Asia
by Grantham Book Services,
Trent Road, Grantham NG31 7XQ

Distributed in the USA
by Publishers Group West,
1700 Fourth Street, Berkeley, CA 94710

Distributed in Australia and New Zealand
by Allen & Unwin Pty Ltd,
PO Box 8500, 83 Alexander Street,
Crows Nest, NSW 2065

Distributed in South Africa by
Jonathan Ball, Office B4, The District,
41 Sir Lowry Road, Woodstock 7925

Distributed in India by Penguin Books India,
7th Floor, Infinity Tower – C, DLF Cyber City,
Gurgaon 122002, Haryana

Distributed in Canada by Publishers Group Canada,
76 Stafford Street, Unit 300
Toronto, Ontario M6J 2S1

ISBN: 978-178578-783-6

Typeset in Gotham by Marie Doherty

Printed and bound in Italy,
by Elcograf S.p.A.

QUARANTINE COMIX

QUARANTINE COMIX

A MEMOIR OF LIFE IN LOCKDOWN

by Rachael Smith

ICON

MAIN CAST

RACHAEL

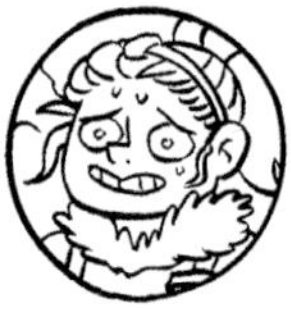

OUR MAIN CHARACTER/NARRATOR. A 35 YEAR OLD CARTOONIST. VERY ANXIOUS! LIKES WINE AND VIDEO GAMES. CRIES A LOT. TRIES HER BEST.

RUFUS

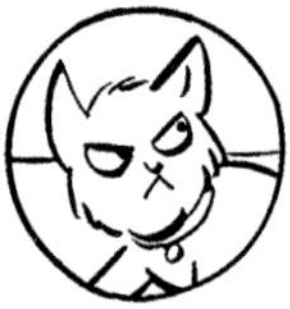

RACHAEL'S CAT/BFF. LIKES A LOT OF ATTENTION. ALSO HATES ATTENTION. IS CONFUSED AS TO WHY THE HUMANS ARE HOME ALL THE TIME THESE DAYS.

IAIN

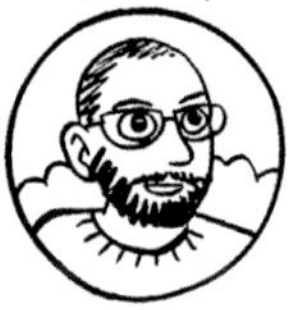

RACHAEL'S HOUSEMATE. AN AMAZING COOK AND MUSICIAN! DOES CLEVER STUFF WITH INSURANCE WHICH RACHAEL DOESN'T REALLY UNDERSTAND.

ROB

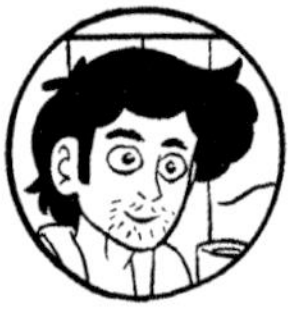

RACHAEL'S BOYFRIEND. CURRENTLY STUCK AWAY FROM RACHAEL DUE TO LOCKDOWN. IS FULL OF KINDNESS AND INTEGRITY. AWESOME ANIMATOR!

• • • • •

HEATHER

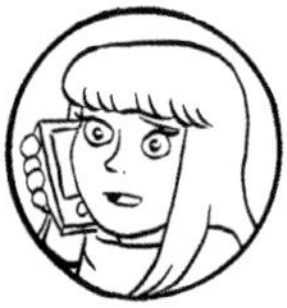

RACHAEL'S BEST (HUMAN) FRIEND. SUPER CLEVER. HAS, LIKE, 5 DEGREES OR SOMETHING. I SHOULD PROBABLY CHECK THAT BEFORE THIS GOES TO PRINT.

BARKY

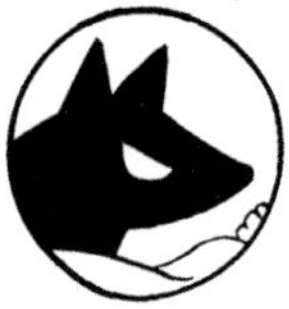

AN IMAGINARY DOG. HE REPRESENTS RACHAEL'S DEPRESSION AND PESSIMISM. TELLS RACHAEL TO DO STUPID THINGS. KIND OF A DICK. SHUT UP, BARKY!

FRIENDLY

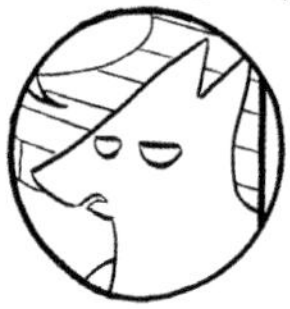

ALSO AN IMAGINARY DOG. SHE REPRESENTS RACHAEL'S COMMON SENSE AND OPTIMISM. TELLS RACHAEL GOOD AND USEFUL THINGS. YAY, FRIENDLY!

PROLOGUE....

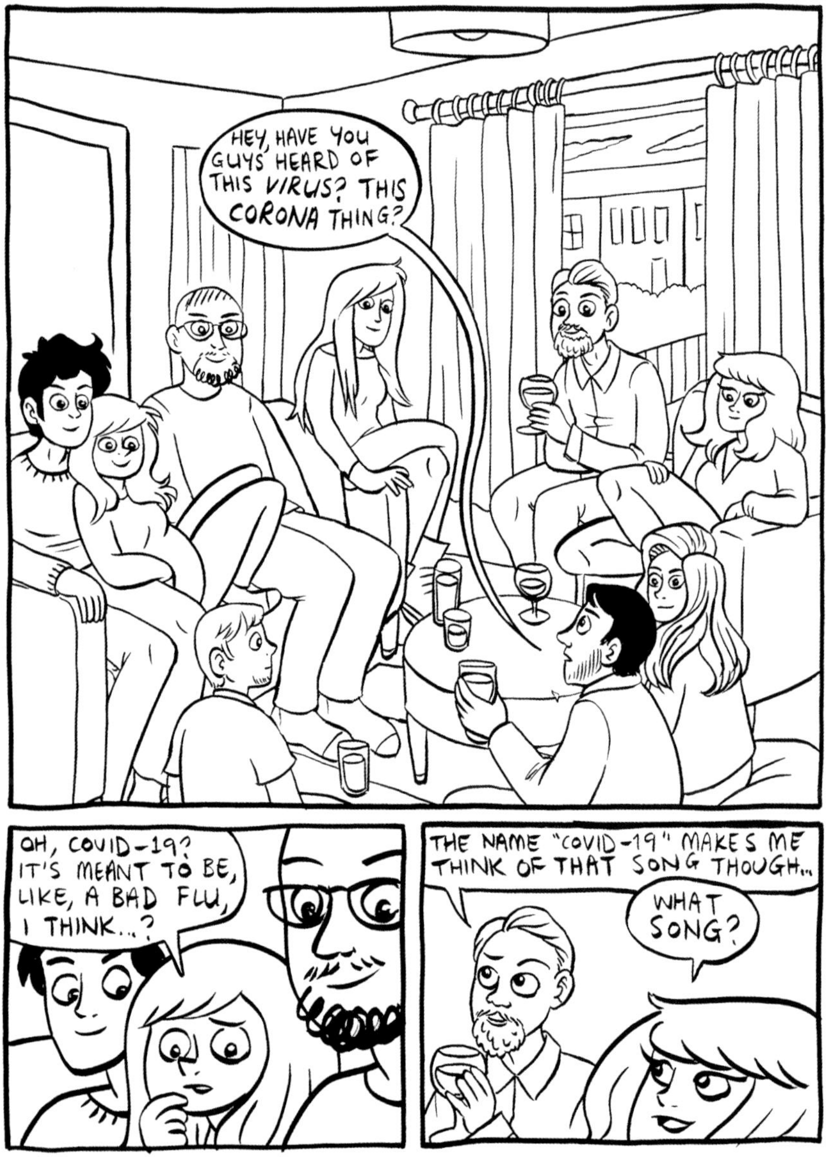
HEY, HAVE YOU GUYS HEARD OF THIS *VIRUS*? THIS *CORONA* THING?
OH, COVID-19? IT'S MEANT TO BE, LIKE, A BAD FLU, I THINK...?
THE NAME "COVID-19" MAKES ME THINK OF THAT SONG THOUGH...
WHAT SONG?

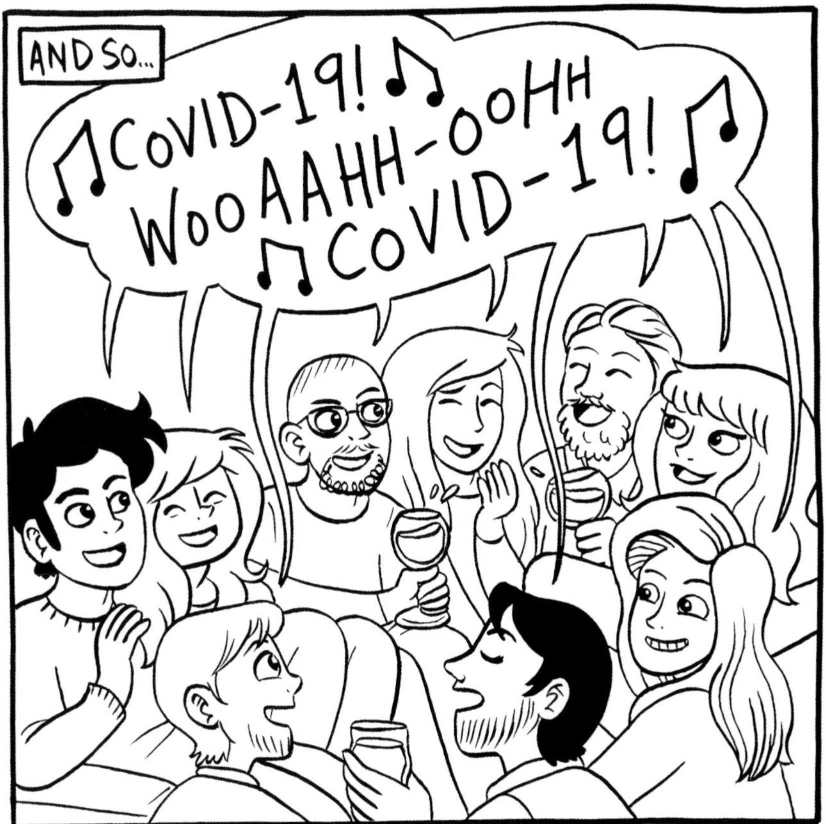
AND SO...
♫COVID-19!♫ WooAAHH-OOHH ♫COVID-19!♫ ♫COVID-19!♫

*SUNG TO THE TUNE OF "COME ON EILEEN" BY DEXYS MIDNIGHT RUNNERS.

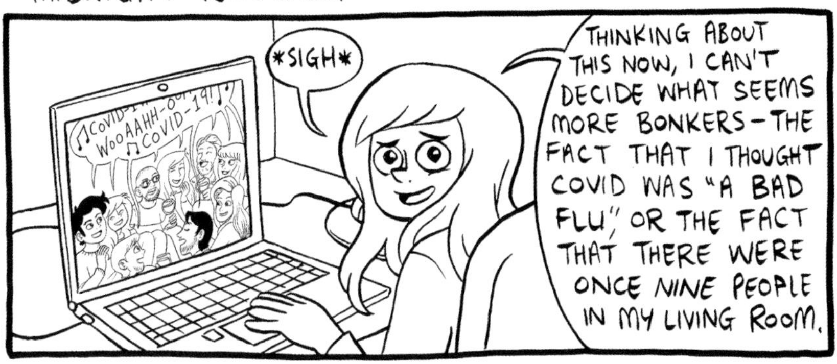
SIGH
THINKING ABOUT THIS NOW, I CAN'T DECIDE WHAT SEEMS MORE BONKERS—THE FACT THAT I THOUGHT COVID WAS "A BAD FLU," OR THE FACT THAT THERE WERE ONCE NINE PEOPLE IN MY LIVING ROOM.

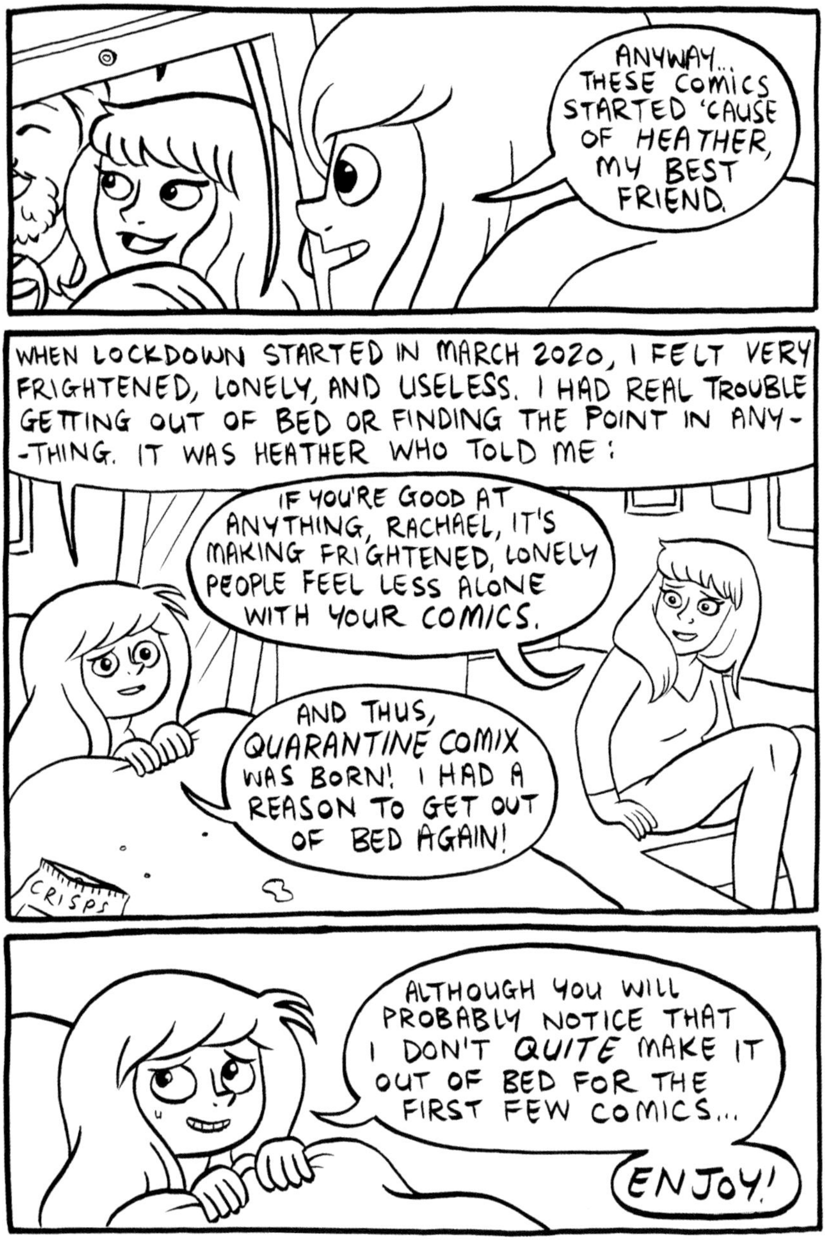
ANYWAY... THESE COMICS STARTED 'CAUSE OF HEATHER, MY BEST FRIEND.
WHEN LOCKDOWN STARTED IN MARCH 2020, I FELT VERY FRIGHTENED, LONELY, AND USELESS. I HAD REAL TROUBLE GETTING OUT OF BED OR FINDING THE POINT IN ANY--THING. IT WAS HEATHER WHO TOLD ME:
IF YOU'RE GOOD AT ANYTHING, RACHAEL, IT'S MAKING FRIGHTENED, LONELY PEOPLE FEEL LESS ALONE WITH YOUR COMICS.
AND THUS, QUARANTINE COMIX WAS BORN! I HAD A REASON TO GET OUT OF BED AGAIN!
CRISPS
ALTHOUGH YOU WILL PROBABLY NOTICE THAT I DON'T QUITE MAKE IT OUT OF BED FOR THE FIRST FEW COMICS...
ENJOY!

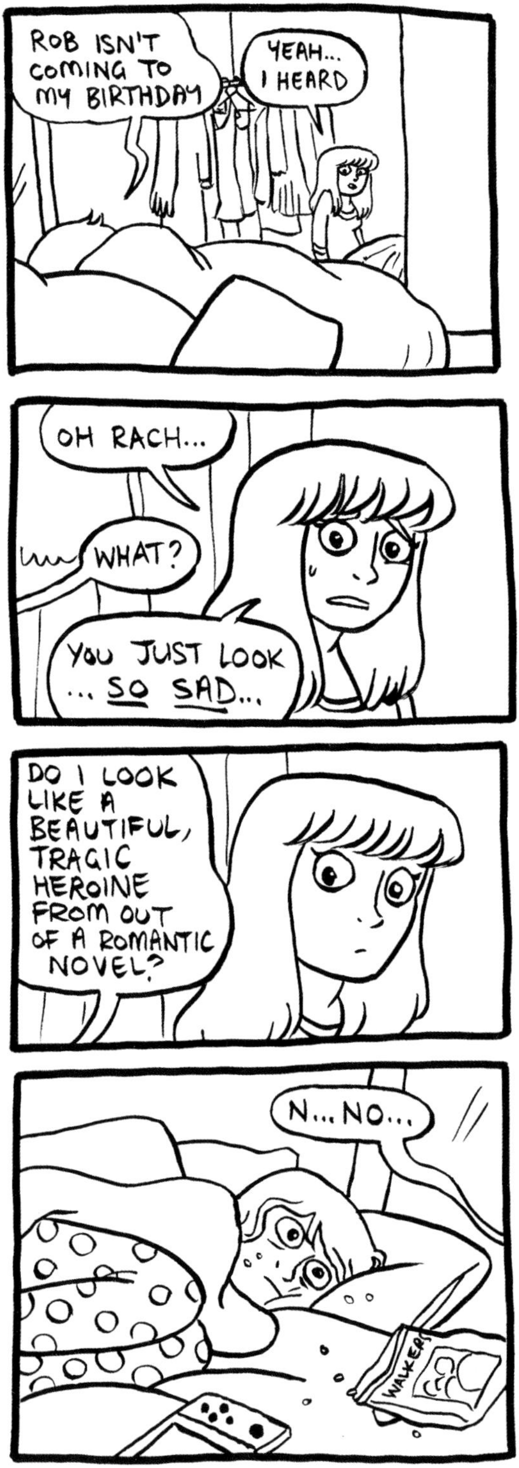
ROB ISN'T COMING TO MY BIRTHDAY
YEAH... I HEARD
OH RACH...
WHAT?
YOU JUST LOOK ... SO SAD...
DO I LOOK LIKE A BEAUTIFUL, TRAGIC HEROINE FROM OUT OF A ROMANTIC NOVEL?
N... NO...
WALKERS

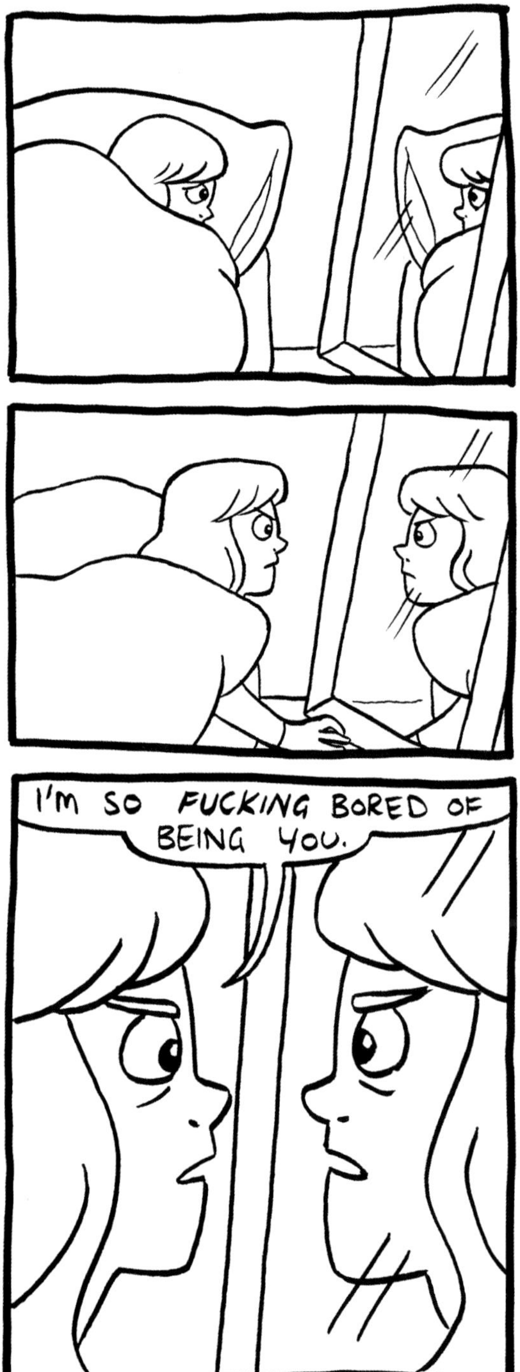
I'M SO FUCKING BORED OF BEING YOU.

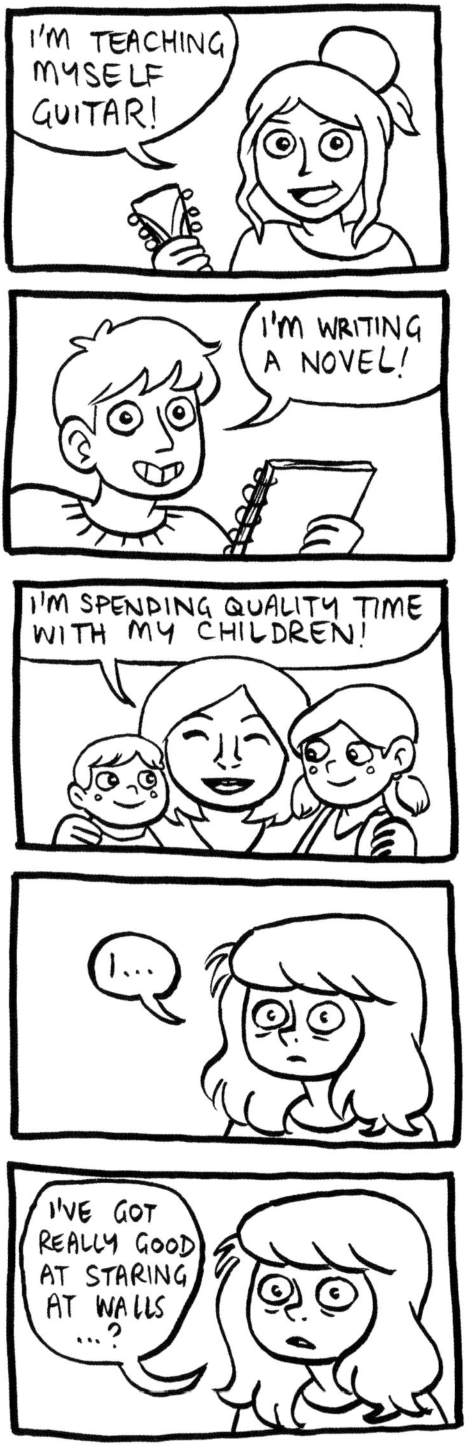
I'M TEACHING MYSELF GUITAR!
I'M WRITING A NOVEL!
I'M SPENDING QUALITY TIME WITH MY CHILDREN!
I...
I'VE GOT REALLY GOOD AT STARING AT WALLS ...?

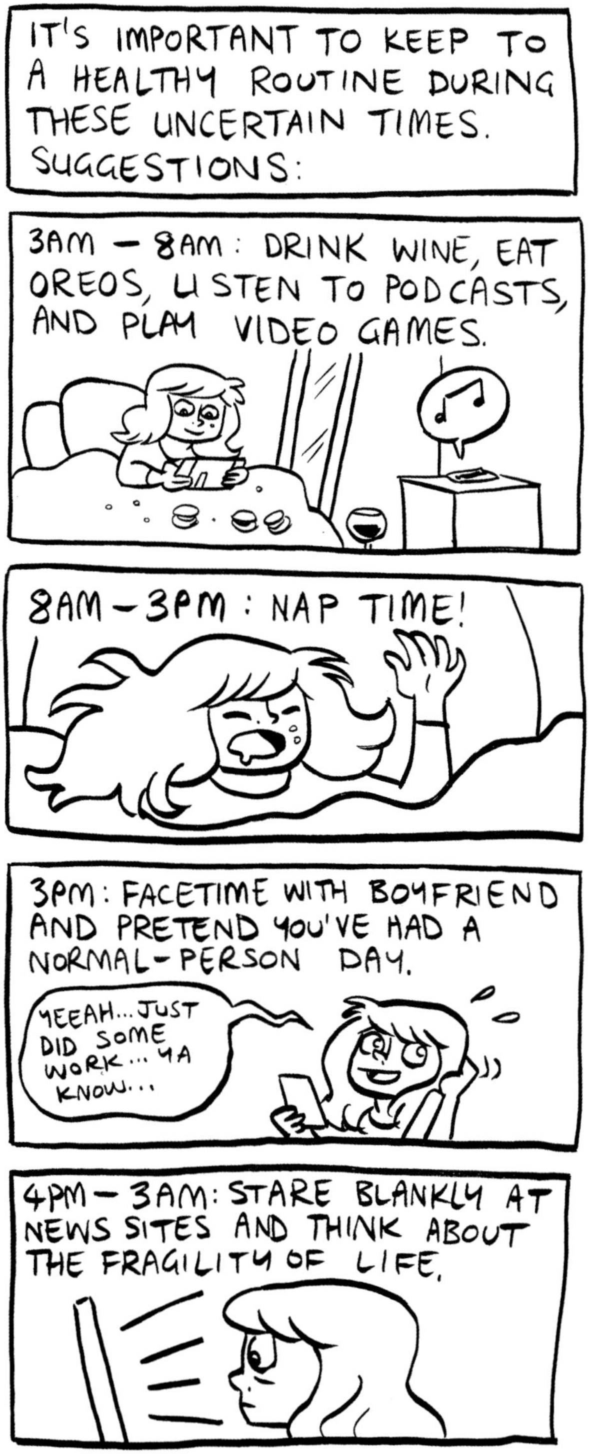
IT'S IMPORTANT TO KEEP TO A HEALTHY ROUTINE DURING THESE UNCERTAIN TIMES. SUGGESTIONS:
3AM – 8AM: DRINK WINE, EAT OREOS, LISTEN TO PODCASTS, AND PLAY VIDEO GAMES.
8AM – 3PM: NAP TIME!
3PM: FACETIME WITH BOYFRIEND AND PRETEND YOU'VE HAD A NORMAL-PERSON DAY.
YEEAH... JUST DID SOME WORK... YA KNOW...
4PM – 3AM: STARE BLANKLY AT NEWS SITES AND THINK ABOUT THE FRAGILITY OF LIFE.

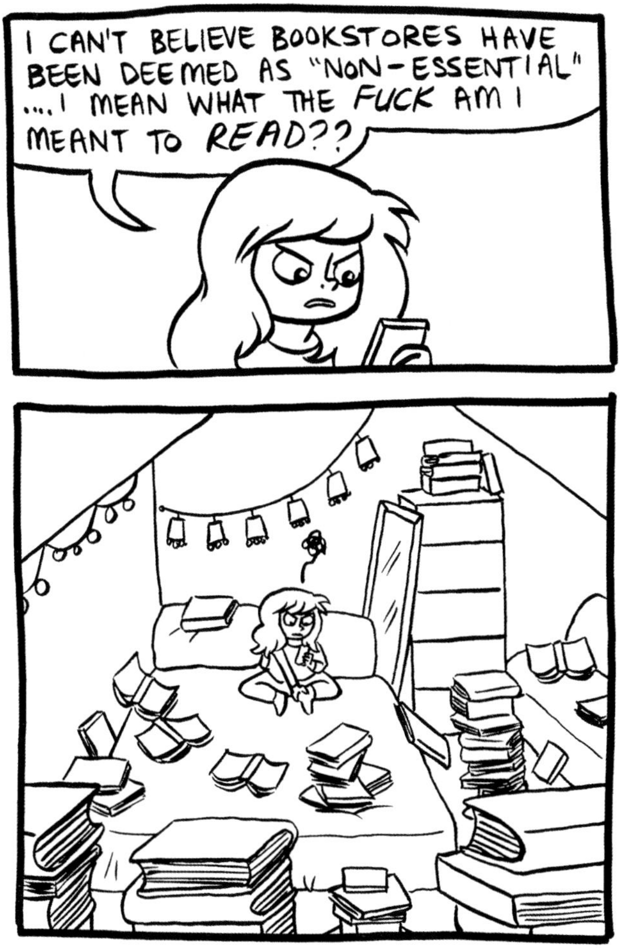
I CAN'T BELIEVE BOOKSTORES HAVE BEEN DEEMED AS "NON-ESSENTIAL" ....I MEAN WHAT THE FUCK AM I MEANT TO READ??

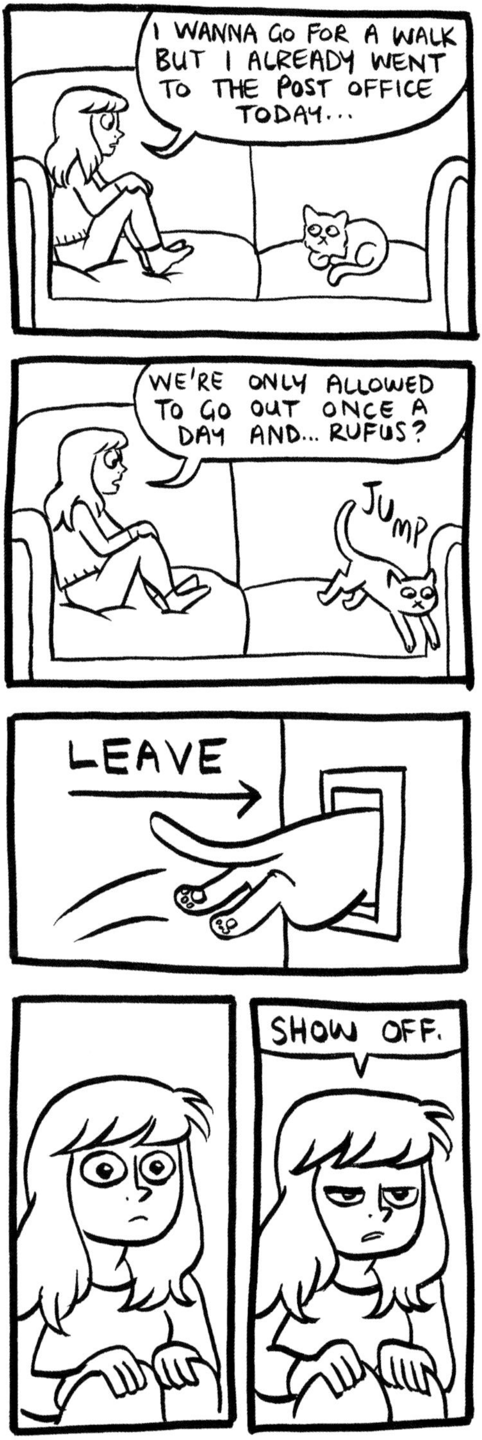
I WANNA GO FOR A WALK BUT I ALREADY WENT TO THE POST OFFICE TODAY...
WE'RE ONLY ALLOWED TO GO OUT ONCE A DAY AND... RUFUS?
JUMP
LEAVE
SHOW OFF.

IAIN (MY HOUSEMATE) AND I WENT FOR A WALK.
SEE THESE TREES?
MM
IN LATE SPRING THEY ALL GO *PINK*. IT'S LIKE WALKING THROUGH A FAIRY TOWN.
WELL... THAT'S SOMETHING TO LOOK FORWARD TO...

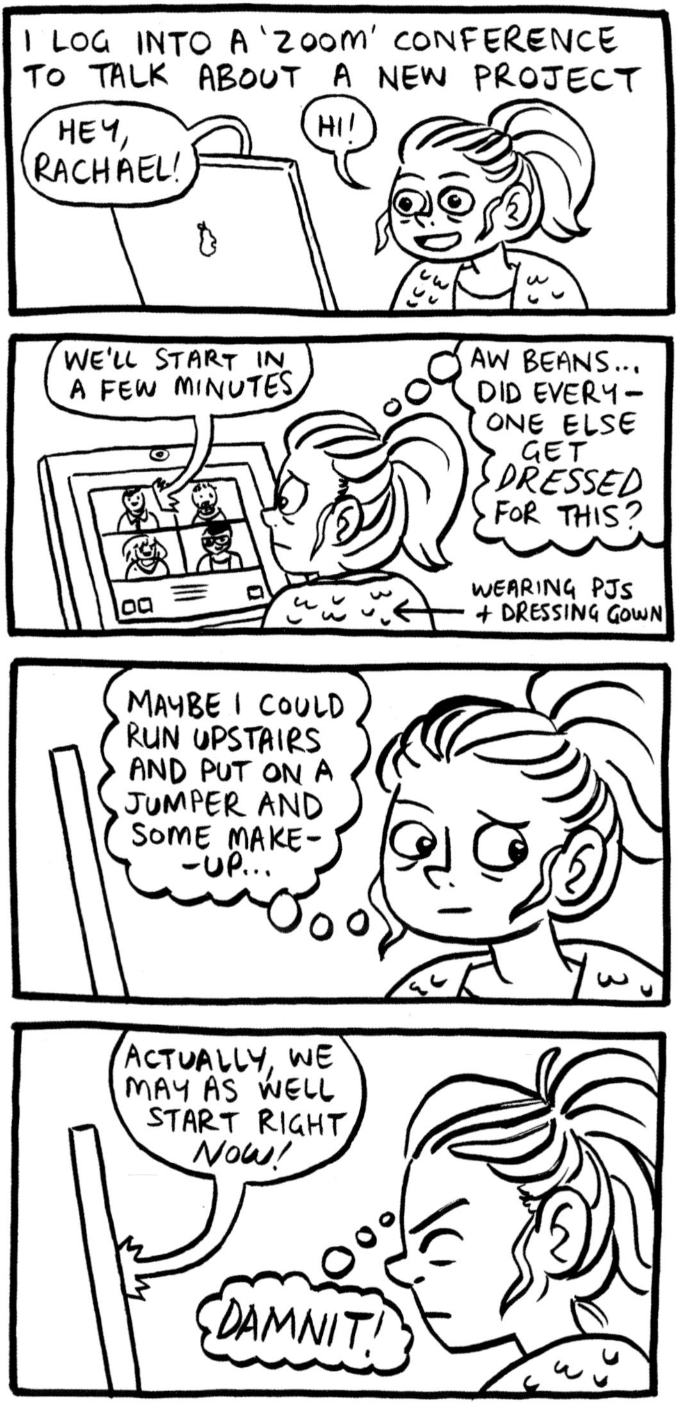
I LOG INTO A 'ZOOM' CONFERENCE TO TALK ABOUT A NEW PROJECT
HEY, RACHAEL!
HI!
WE'LL START IN A FEW MINUTES
AW BEANS... DID EVERY-ONE ELSE GET DRESSED FOR THIS?
WEARING PJs + DRESSING GOWN
MAYBE I COULD RUN UPSTAIRS AND PUT ON A JUMPER AND SOME MAKE--UP...
ACTUALLY, WE MAY AS WELL START RIGHT NOW!
DAMNIT!

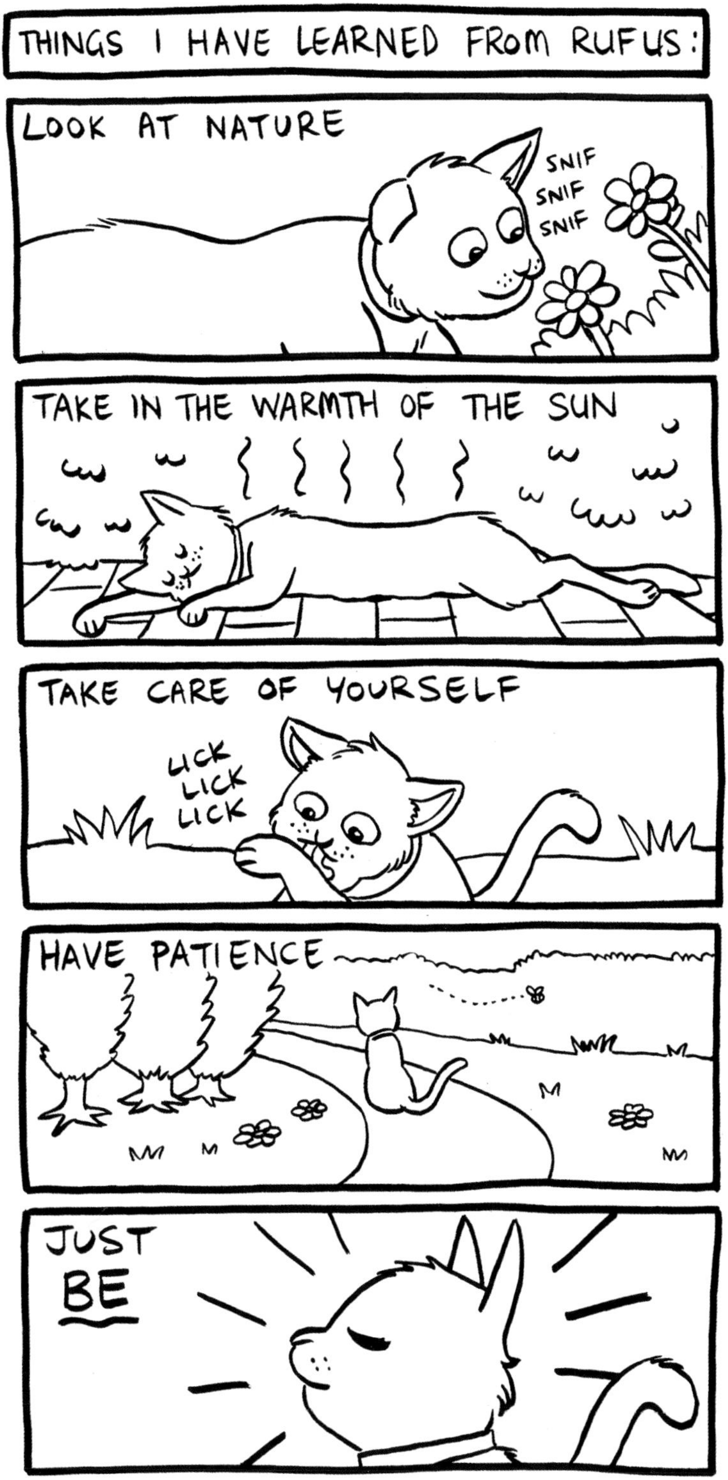

THINGS I HAVE LEARNED FROM RUFUS:
LOOK AT NATURE
SNIF
SNIF
SNIF
TAKE IN THE WARMTH OF THE SUN
TAKE CARE OF YOURSELF
LICK
LICK
LICK
HAVE PATIENCE
JUST
BE

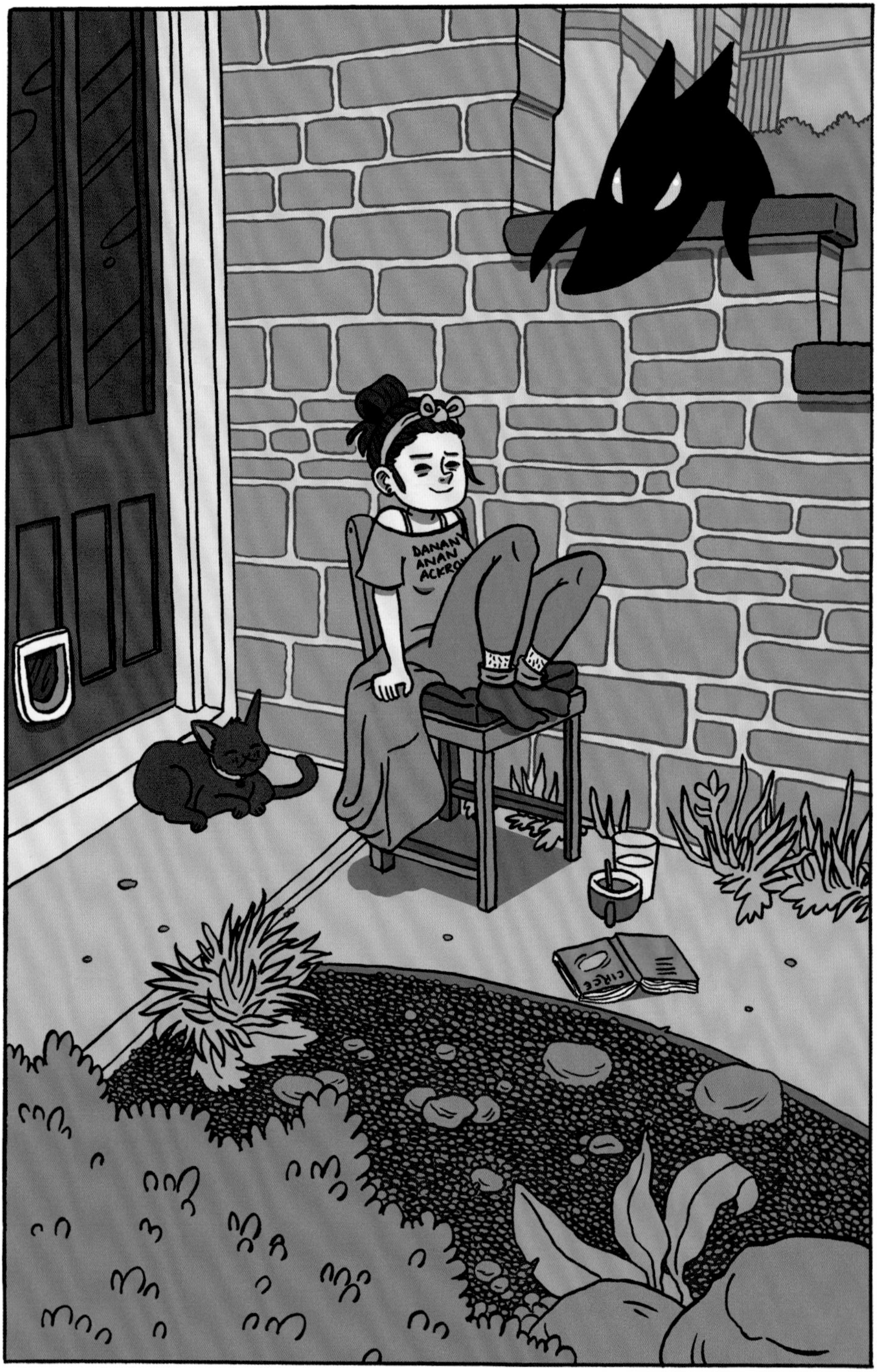
CIRCE

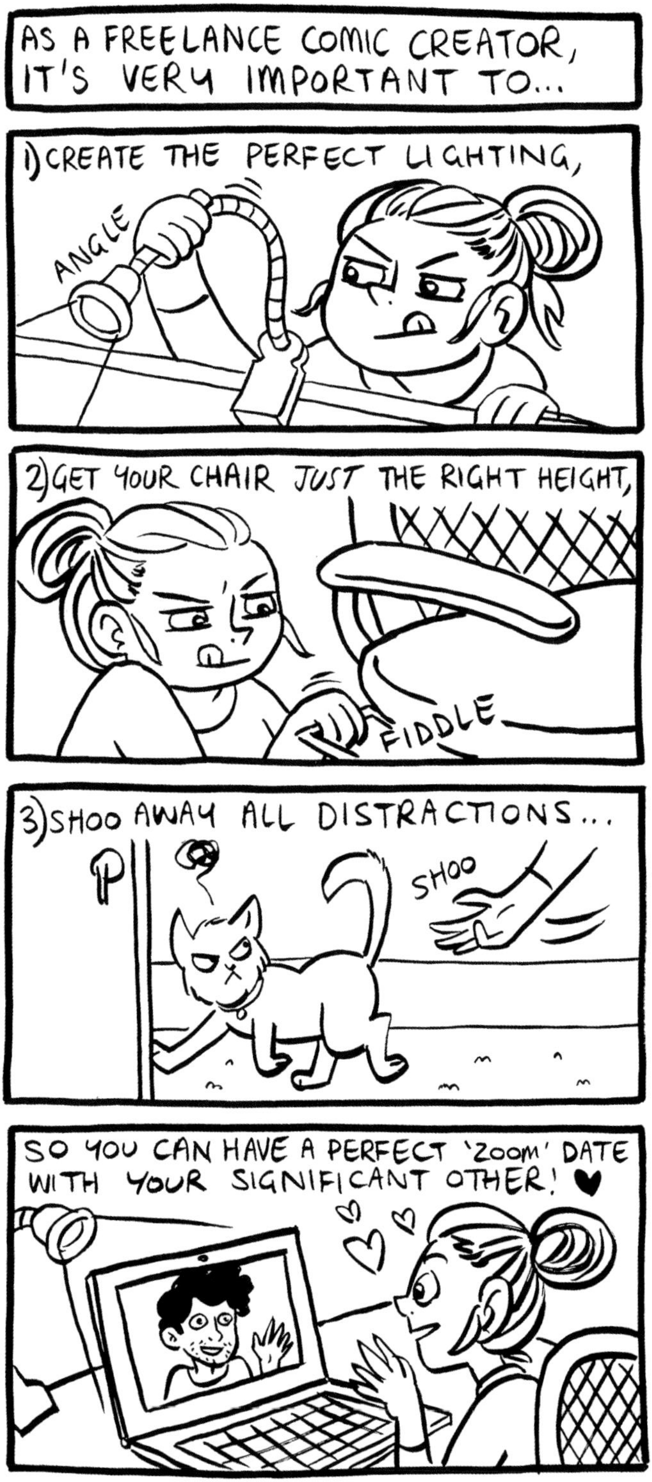
AS A FREELANCE COMIC CREATOR, IT'S VERY IMPORTANT TO...
1) CREATE THE PERFECT LIGHTING,
ANGLE
2) GET YOUR CHAIR JUST THE RIGHT HEIGHT,
FIDDLE
3) SHOO AWAY ALL DISTRACTIONS...
SHOO
SO YOU CAN HAVE A PERFECT 'ZOOM' DATE WITH YOUR SIGNIFICANT OTHER! ♥

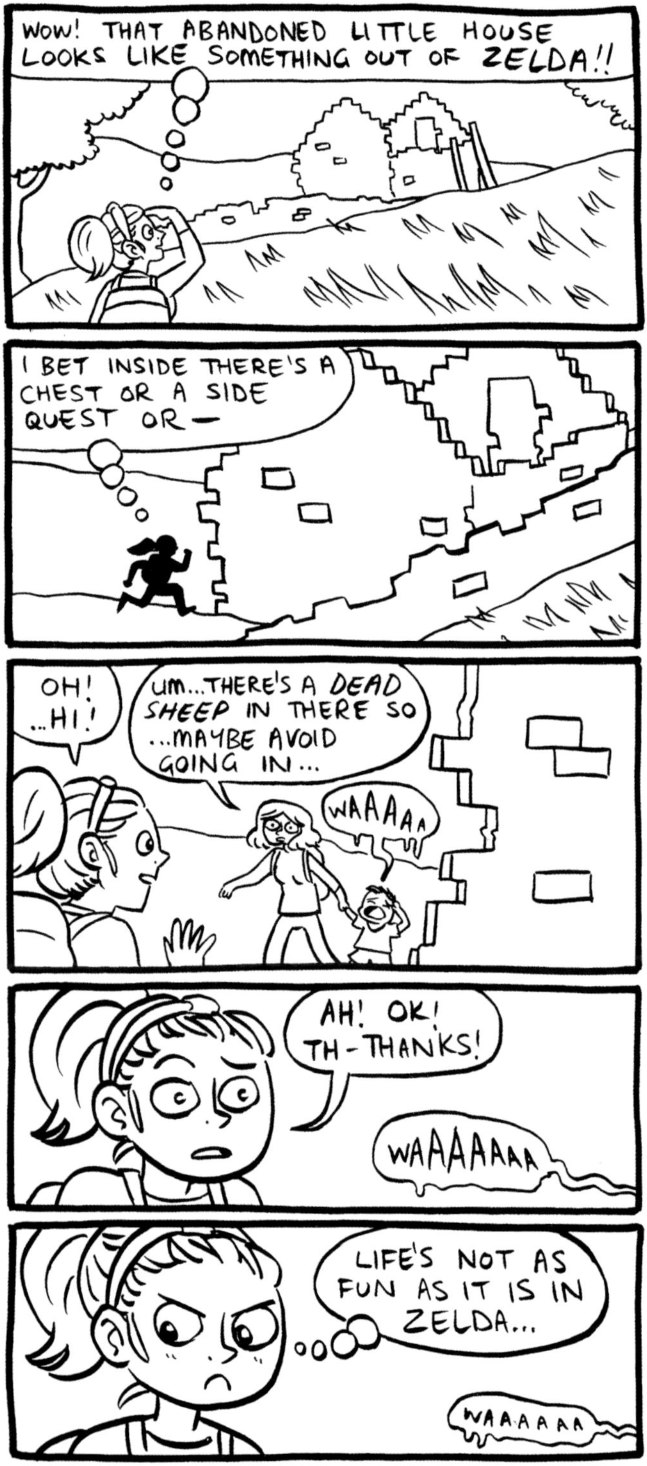
WOW! THAT ABANDONED LITTLE HOUSE LOOKS LIKE SOMETHING OUT OF ZELDA!!
I BET INSIDE THERE'S A CHEST OR A SIDE QUEST OR—
OH! ...HI!
UM...THERE'S A DEAD SHEEP IN THERE SO ...MAYBE AVOID GOING IN...
WAAAAA
AH! OK! TH-THANKS!
WAAAAAAA
LIFE'S NOT AS FUN AS IT IS IN ZELDA...
WAAAAAA

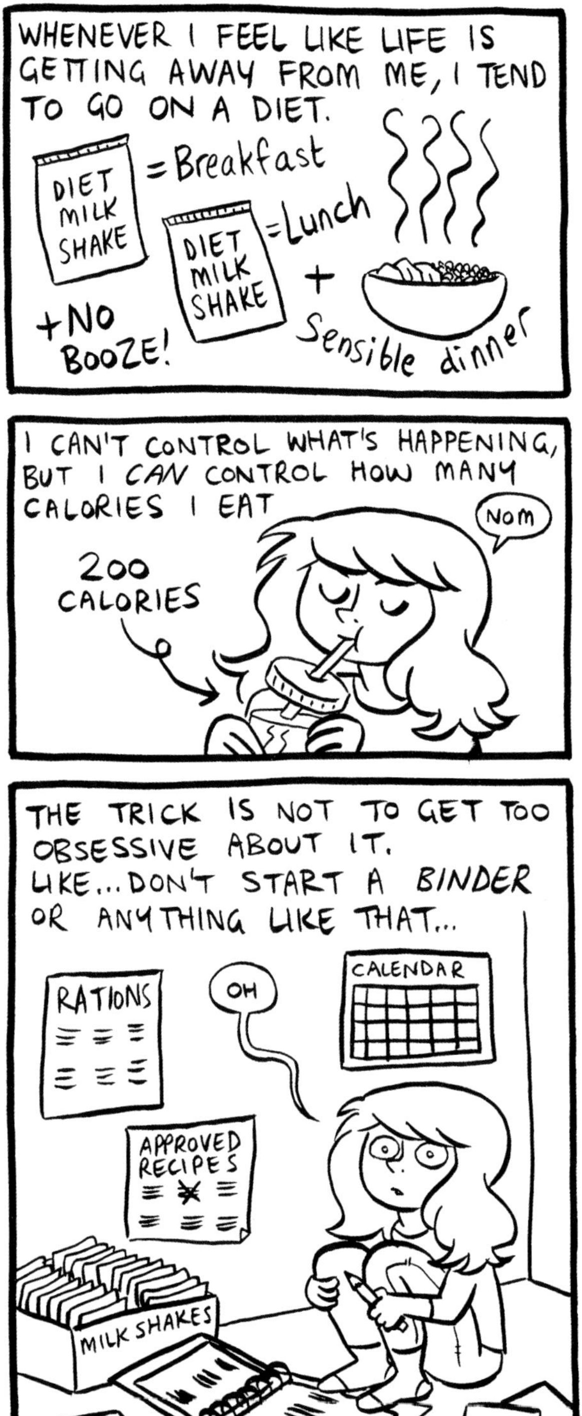
WHENEVER I FEEL LIKE LIFE IS GETTING AWAY FROM ME, I TEND TO GO ON A DIET.
DIET MILK SHAKE
=Breakfast
DIET MILK SHAKE
=Lunch
+
Sensible dinner
+NO BOOZE!
I CAN'T CONTROL WHAT'S HAPPENING, BUT I *CAN* CONTROL HOW MANY CALORIES I EAT
NOM
200 CALORIES
THE TRICK IS NOT TO GET TOO OBSESSIVE ABOUT IT.
LIKE... DON'T START A *BINDER* OR ANYTHING LIKE THAT...
OH
RATIONS
CALENDAR
APPROVED RECIPES
MILK SHAKES

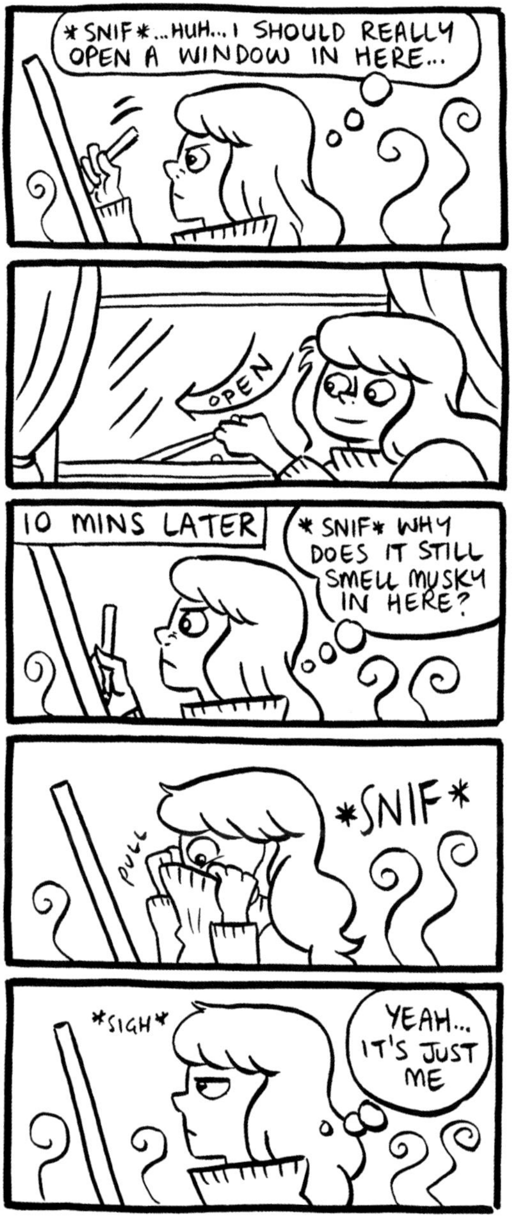
SNIF...HUH...I SHOULD REALLY OPEN A WINDOW IN HERE...
OPEN
10 MINS LATER
SNIF WHY DOES IT STILL SMELL MUSKY IN HERE?
PULL
SNIF
SIGH
YEAH... IT'S JUST ME

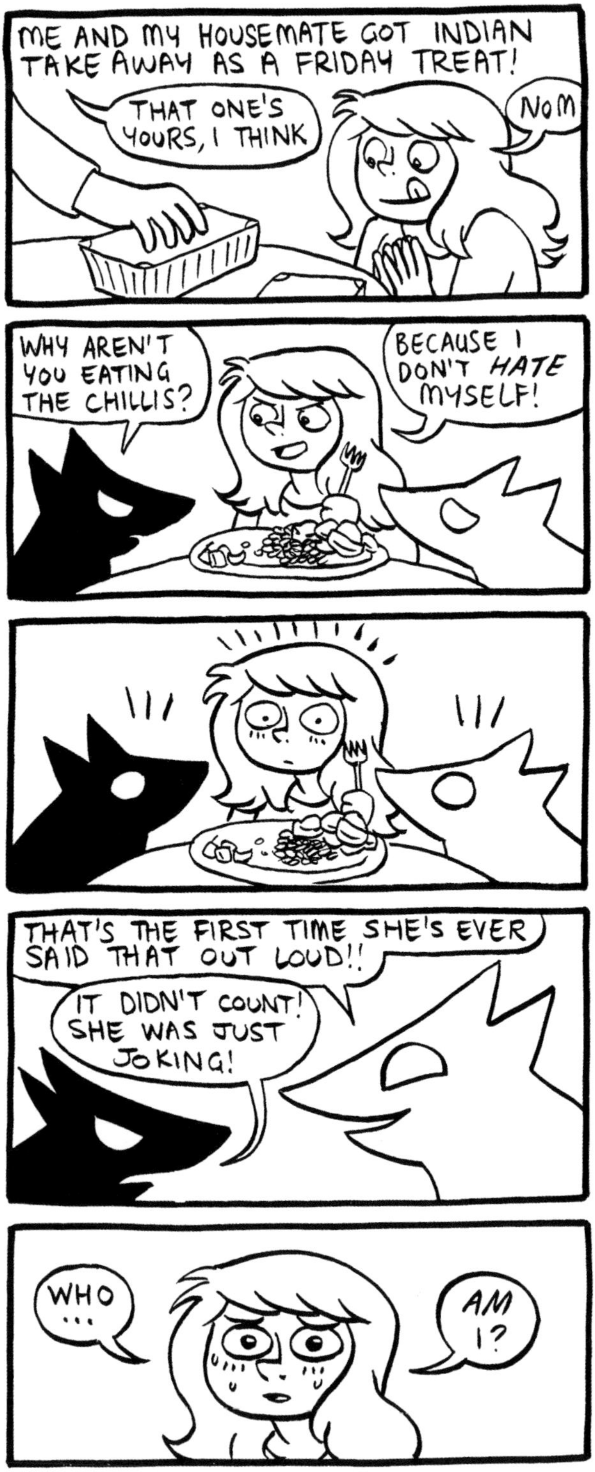
ME AND MY HOUSEMATE GOT INDIAN TAKE AWAY AS A FRIDAY TREAT!
THAT ONE'S YOURS, I THINK
NOM
WHY AREN'T YOU EATING THE CHILLIS?
BECAUSE I DON'T HATE MYSELF!
THAT'S THE FIRST TIME SHE'S EVER SAID THAT OUT LOUD!!
IT DIDN'T COUNT! SHE WAS JUST JOKING!
WHO ...
AM I?

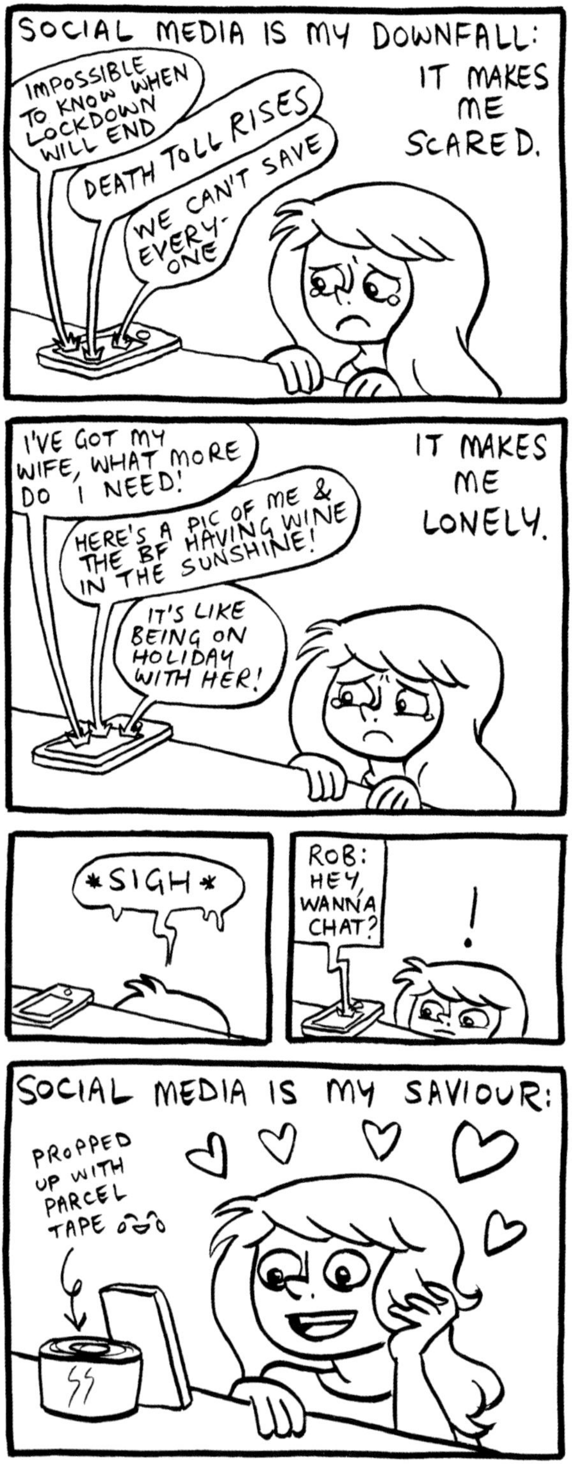
SOCIAL MEDIA IS MY DOWNFALL:
IMPOSSIBLE TO KNOW WHEN LOCKDOWN WILL END
DEATH TOLL RISES
WE CAN'T SAVE EVERY-ONE
IT MAKES ME SCARED.
I'VE GOT MY WIFE, WHAT MORE DO I NEED!
HERE'S A PIC OF ME & THE BF HAVING WINE IN THE SUNSHINE!
IT'S LIKE BEING ON HOLIDAY WITH HER!
IT MAKES ME LONELY.
SIGH
ROB: HEY, WANNA CHAT?
!
SOCIAL MEDIA IS MY SAVIOUR:
PROPPED UP WITH PARCEL TAPE

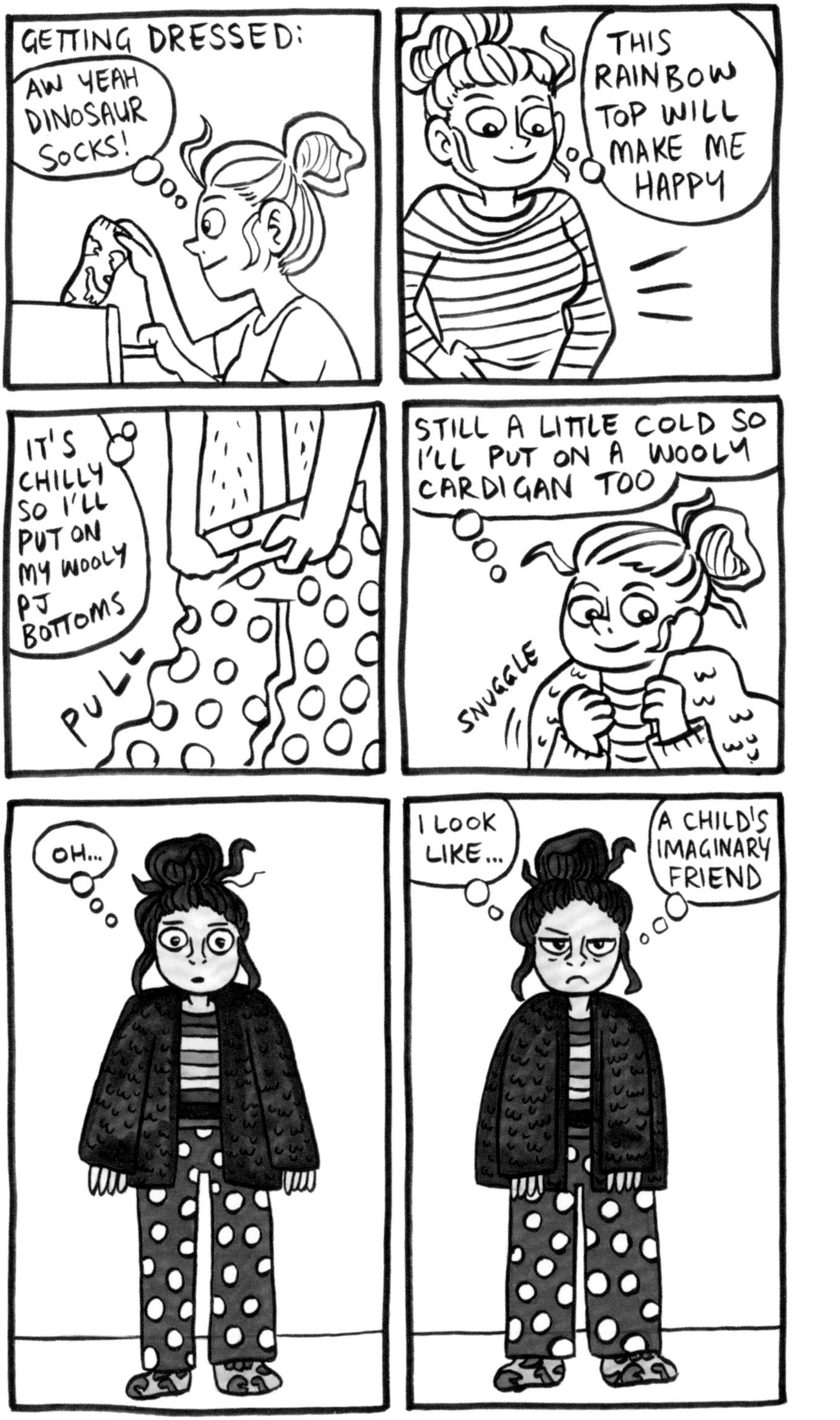
GETTING DRESSED:
AW YEAH DINOSAUR SOCKS!
THIS RAINBOW TOP WILL MAKE ME HAPPY
IT'S CHILLY SO I'LL PUT ON MY WOOLY PJ BOTTOMS
PULL
STILL A LITTLE COLD SO I'LL PUT ON A WOOLY CARDIGAN TOO
SNUGGLE
OH...
I LOOK LIKE...
A CHILD'S IMAGINARY FRIEND

WHEN YOU GO OUT IN THE WOODS IT'S LIKE THERE'S NO PANDEMIC AT ALL
NATURE JUST GETS ON WITH IT.
NATURE IS AMAZING!
WAAAAK!!! WAAAK!
OH MY GOD... THREE BOY DUCKS ARE ALL TRYING TO RAPE THAT ONE GIRL DUCK ...
WAAAAK!!
NATURE IS HORRIBLE
WAAAK...

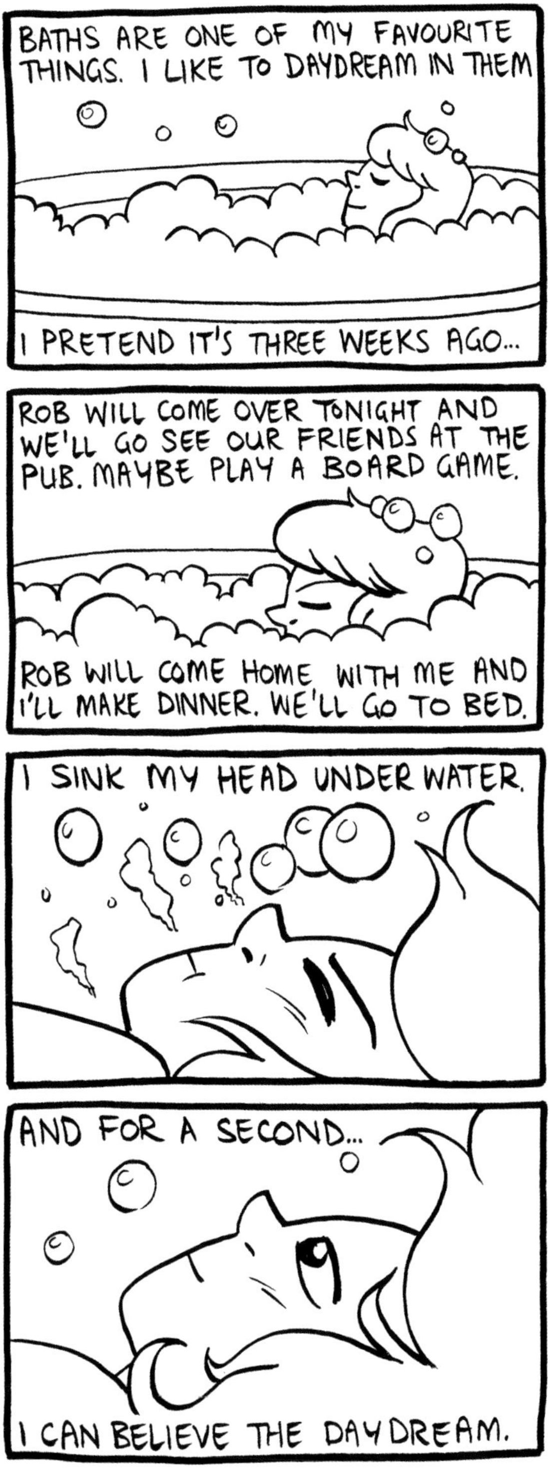
BATHS ARE ONE OF MY FAVOURITE THINGS. I LIKE TO DAYDREAM IN THEM
I PRETEND IT'S THREE WEEKS AGO...
ROB WILL COME OVER TONIGHT AND WE'LL GO SEE OUR FRIENDS AT THE PUB. MAYBE PLAY A BOARD GAME.
ROB WILL COME HOME WITH ME AND I'LL MAKE DINNER. WE'LL GO TO BED.
I SINK MY HEAD UNDER WATER.
AND FOR A SECOND...
I CAN BELIEVE THE DAYDREAM.

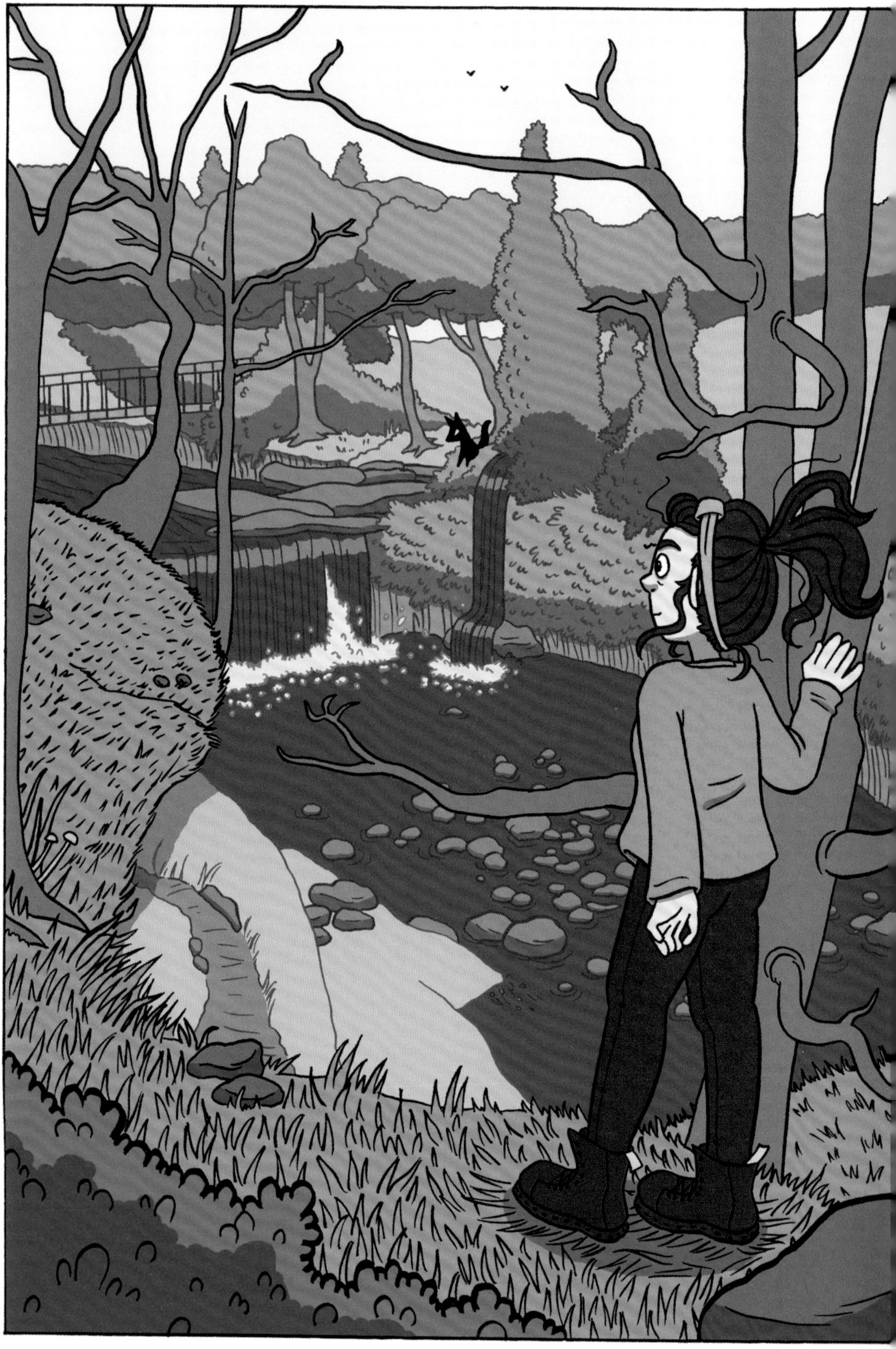

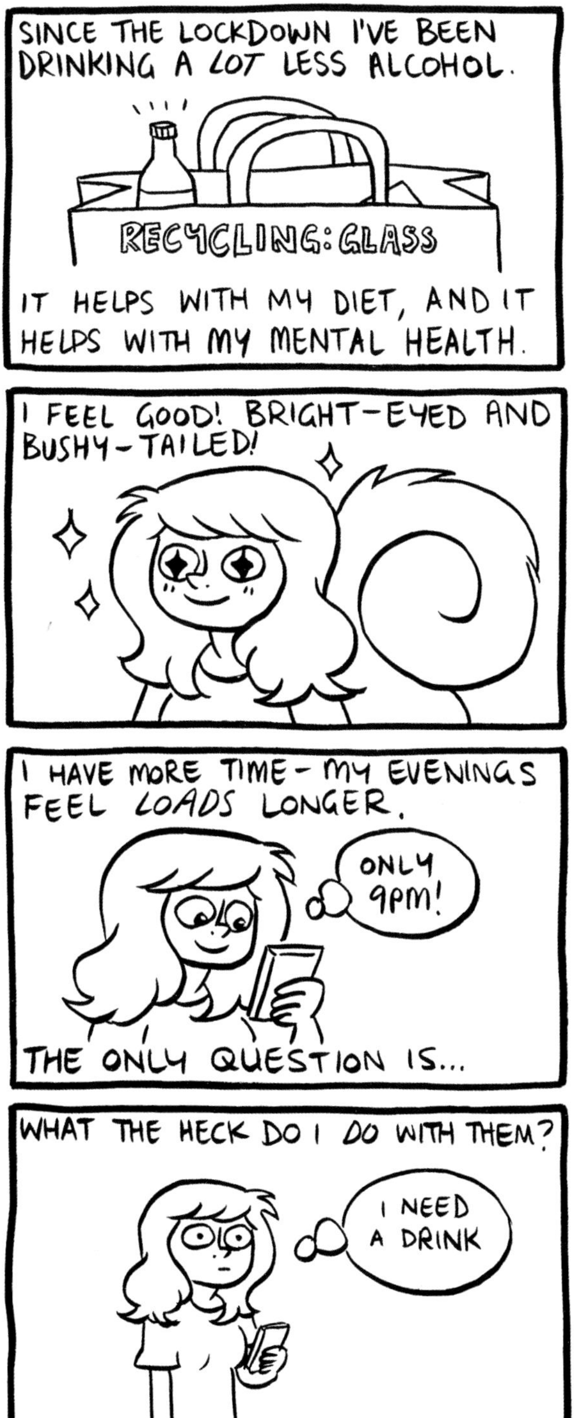
SINCE THE LOCKDOWN I'VE BEEN DRINKING A *LOT* LESS ALCOHOL.
RECYCLING: GLASS
IT HELPS WITH MY DIET, AND IT HELPS WITH MY MENTAL HEALTH.
I FEEL GOOD! BRIGHT-EYED AND BUSHY-TAILED!
I HAVE MORE TIME - MY EVENINGS FEEL *LOADS* LONGER.
ONLY 9PM!
THE ONLY QUESTION IS...
WHAT THE HECK DO I *DO* WITH THEM?
I NEED A DRINK

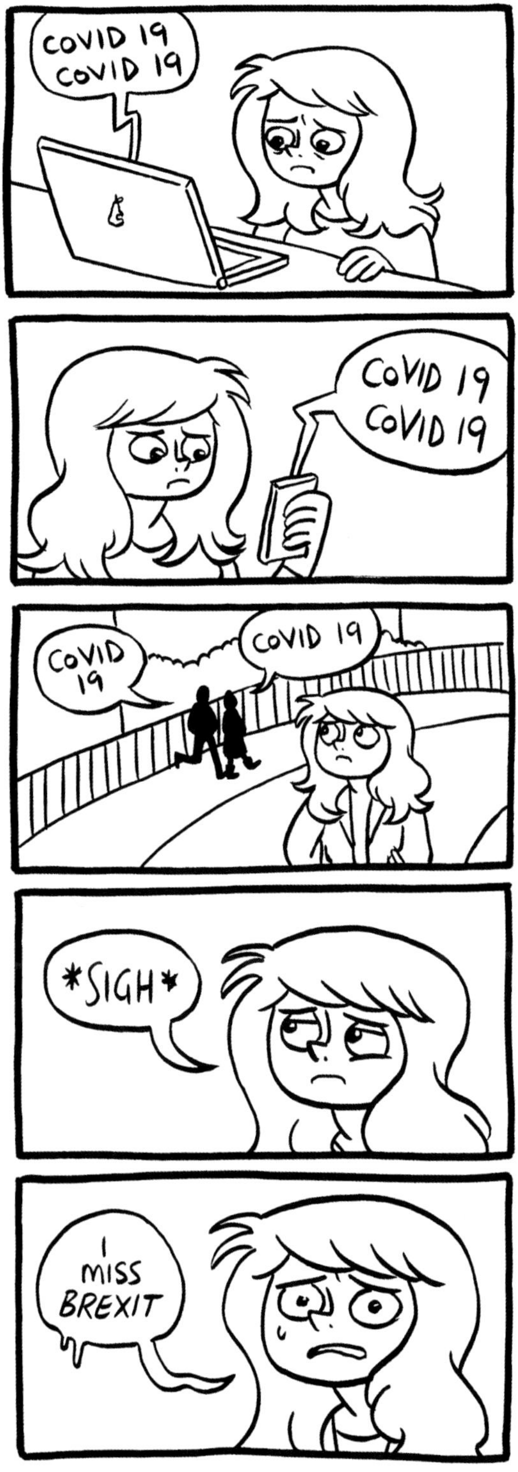
COVID 19
COVID 19
COVID 19
COVID 19
COVID 19
COVID 19
SIGH
I MISS BREXIT

I LIKE TO PUT LITTLE MODEL ANIMALS IN MY GROWING PLANTS. IT'S LIKE THEY ARE WATCHING OVER THEM.
DINOSAUR
GUINEA PIG
♪
YOU ARE 35
PLACE
♪
CORRECT

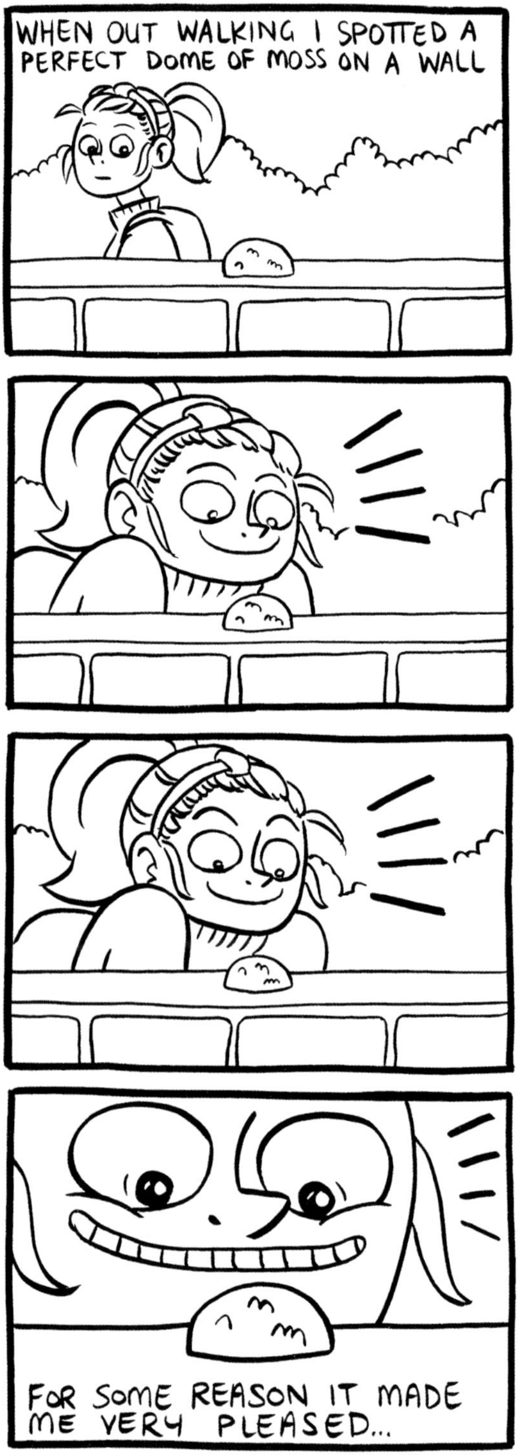
WHEN OUT WALKING I SPOTTED A PERFECT DOME OF MOSS ON A WALL
FOR SOME REASON IT MADE ME VERY PLEASED...

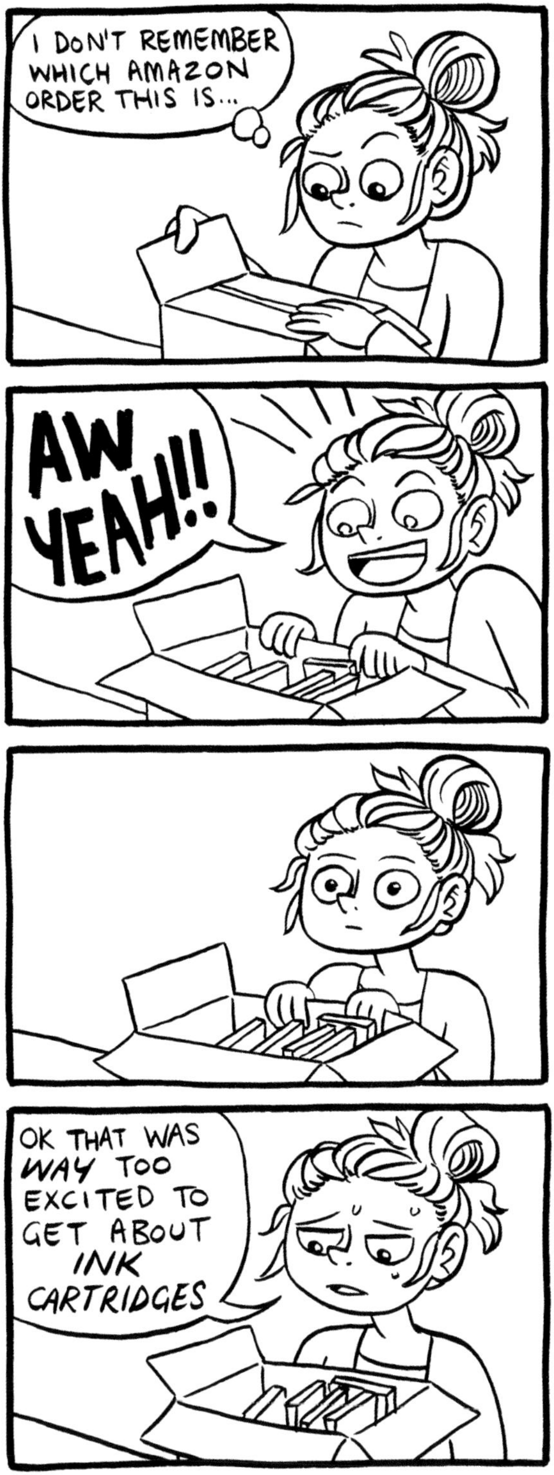
I DON'T REMEMBER WHICH AMAZON ORDER THIS IS...
AW YEAH!!
OK THAT WAS WAY TOO EXCITED TO GET ABOUT INK CARTRIDGES

I HAVE A PHONECALL WITH MY AGENT AT 2PM... I DON'T REALLY WANNA CHANGE OUT OF MY PJS... BUT I SHOULD PROBABLY DO SOMETHING TO FEEL A BIT MORE... PROFESSIONAL...
BY JOVE I'VE GOT IT!
LIPSTICK!
A BRA!
HELLO!
WELL PROFESSIONAL VOICE

I TAKE A BREAK ON ONE OF MY WALKS TO WATCH SOME TINY LITTLE LAMBS PLAY ABOUT.
LIFE, APPARENTLY, GOES ON
HELLO

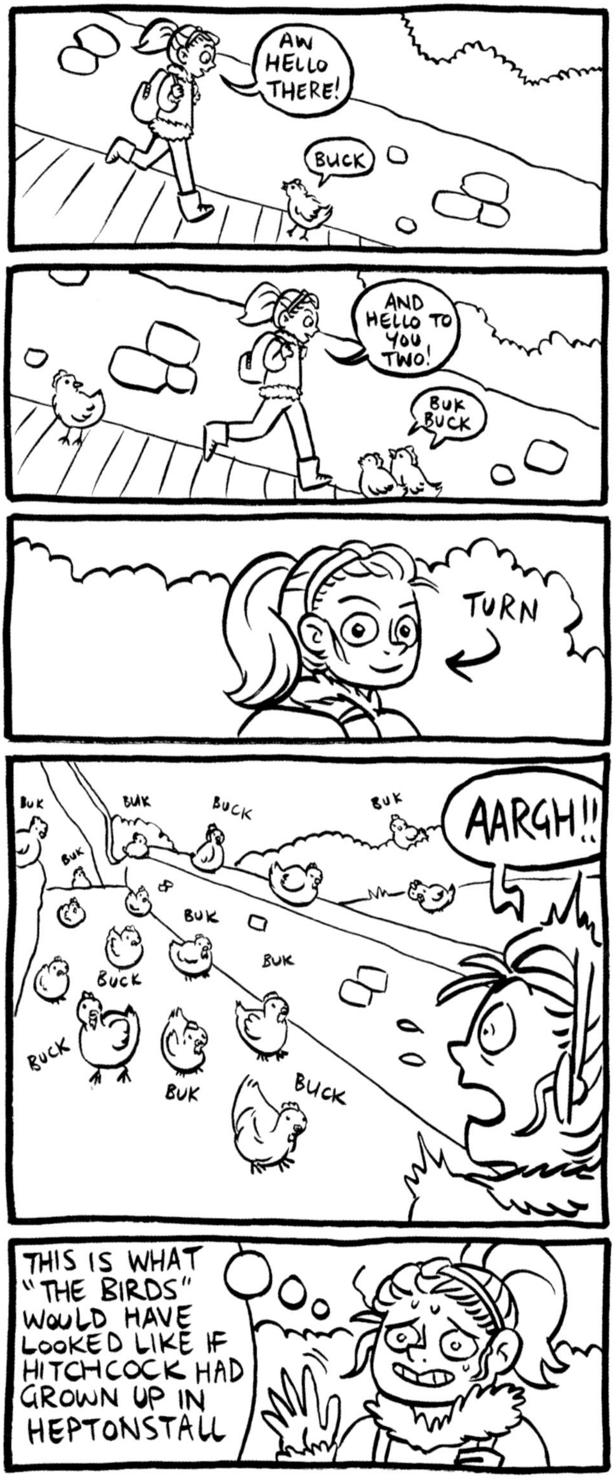
AW HELLO THERE!
BUCK
AND HELLO TO YOU TWO!
BUK BUCK
TURN
BUK
BUK
BUCK
BUK
BUK
AARGH!!
BUK
BUK
BUCK
BUCK
BUK
BUCK
THIS IS WHAT "THE BIRDS" WOULD HAVE LOOKED LIKE IF HITCHCOCK HAD GROWN UP IN HEPTONSTALL

I FEEL SAD.
THEN I FEEL GUILTY FOR FEELING SAD BECAUSE SOME FOLK HAVE IT SO MUCH WORSE THAN I DO.
THEN I FEEL OVERWHELMING PITY FOR THOSE FOLK
NOT GETTING UP TODAY, THEN?
PITY
GUILT
SADNESS

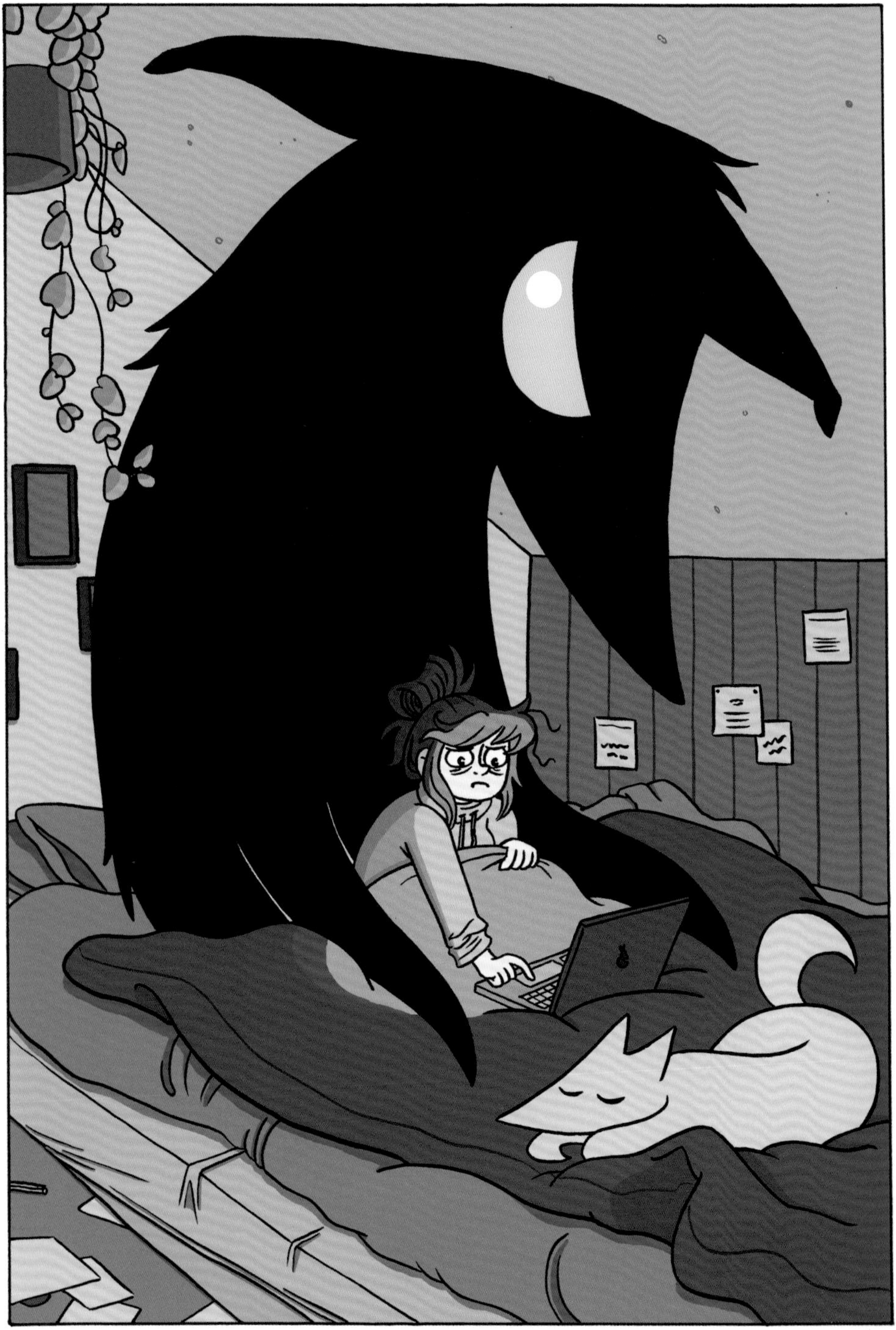

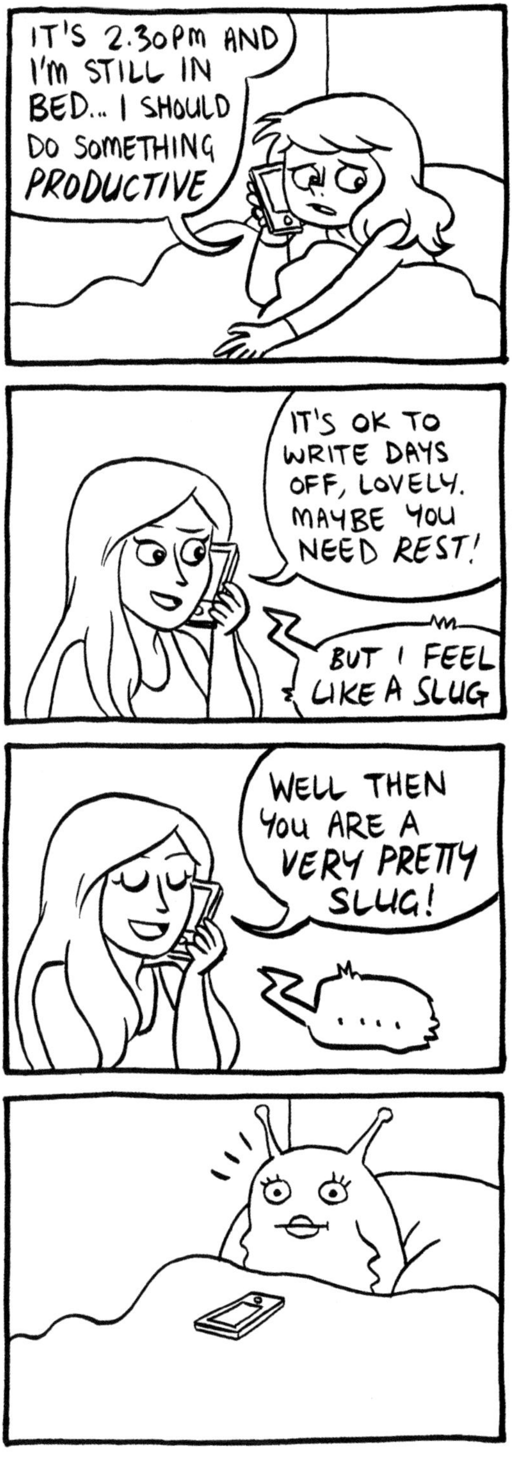
IT'S 2.30PM AND I'M STILL IN BED... I SHOULD DO SOMETHING PRODUCTIVE
IT'S OK TO WRITE DAYS OFF, LOVELY. MAYBE YOU NEED REST!
BUT I FEEL LIKE A SLUG
WELL THEN YOU ARE A VERY PRETTY SLUG!
....

MY FRIEND LUCY SENT ME
SOME SEEDS IN THE POST
AND I FINALLY GOT AROUND
TO POTTING THEM!

THERE'S SOMETHING, ALMOST
REBELLIOUS, ABOUT PLANTING
AND NURTURING THINGS IN
THESE TIMES.

EVEN NOW, THINGS CAN
STILL GROW AND THRIVE.

NOT KNOWING WHEN I'LL GET TO SEE ROB AGAIN IS PRETTY UNBEARABLE.
I TORTURE MYSELF BY LOOKING THROUGH OLD MESSAGES WHERE I'M EXPLAINING WHY I CAN'T HANG OUT WITH HIM.
"I HAVE WORK TO DO TONIGHT, HUN, CAN WE TAKE A RAINCHECK?"
BEING ABLE TO SEE HIM WHENEVER I WANTED SEEMS LIKE SUCH A PRIVILEGE NOW.
I TOOK IT FOR GRANTED.

OLD WAY OF CHOOSING WHAT TO WEAR:
SNIF
SMELLS WEIRD. IN THE WASH YOU GO!
NEW WAY OF CHOOSING WHAT TO WEAR:
SNIF
SMELLS WEIRD ...BUT IF ANYONE SAYS ANYTHING I'LL JUST TELL THEM TO MOVE 6 FEET AWAY...

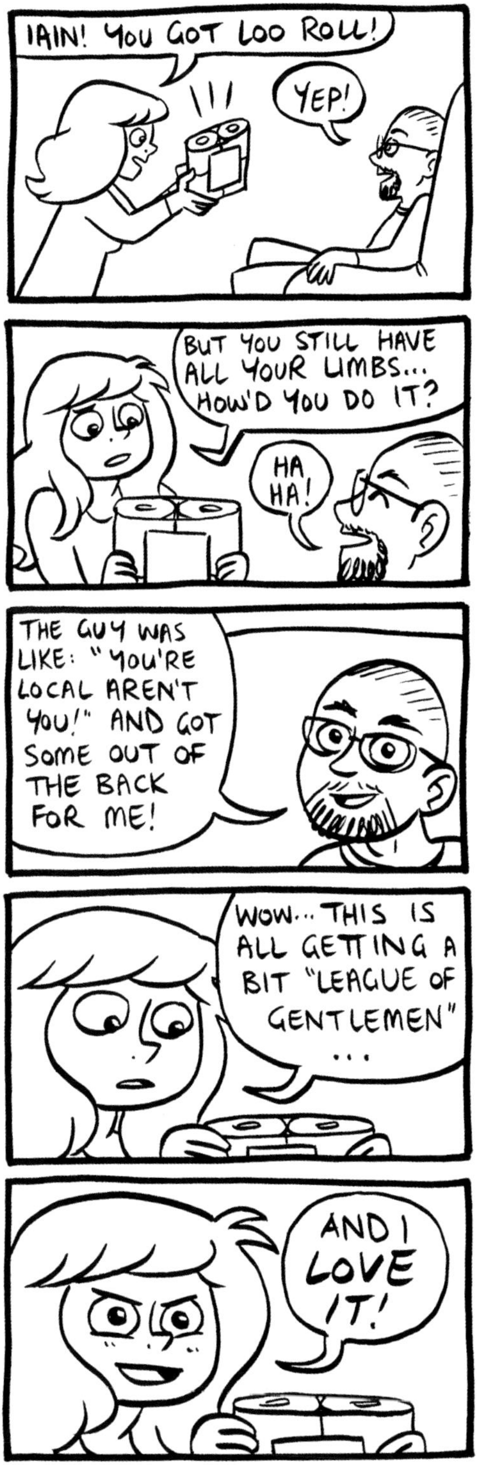
IAIN! YOU GOT LOO ROLL!
YEP!
BUT YOU STILL HAVE ALL YOUR LIMBS... HOW'D YOU DO IT?
HA HA!
THE GUY WAS LIKE: "YOU'RE LOCAL AREN'T YOU!" AND GOT SOME OUT OF THE BACK FOR ME!
WOW... THIS IS ALL GETTING A BIT "LEAGUE OF GENTLEMEN" ...
AND I LOVE IT!

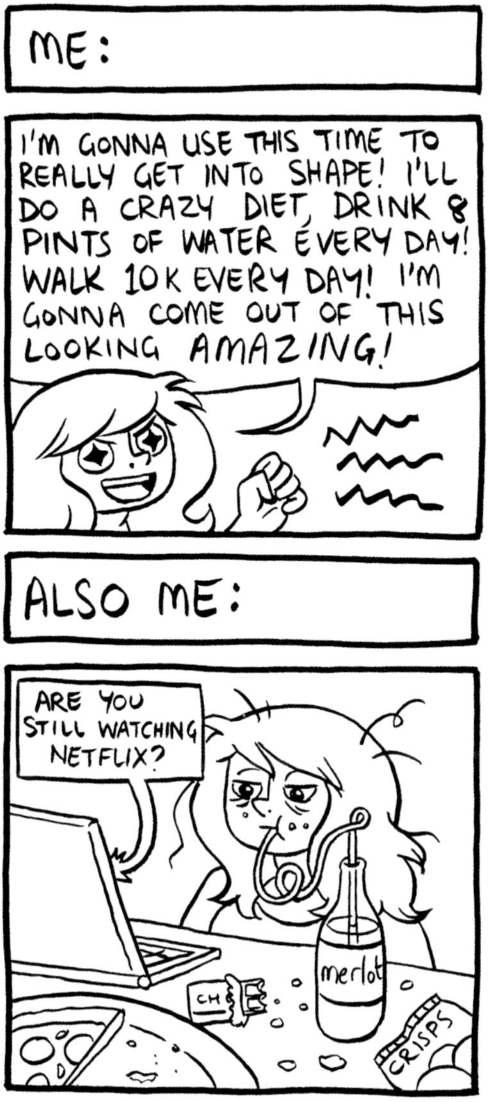
ME:
I'M GONNA USE THIS TIME TO REALLY GET INTO SHAPE! I'LL DO A CRAZY DIET, DRINK 8 PINTS OF WATER EVERY DAY! WALK 10K EVERY DAY! I'M GONNA COME OUT OF THIS LOOKING AMAZING!
ALSO ME:
ARE YOU STILL WATCHING NETFLIX?
merlot
CH
CRISPS

ON SUNNY DAYS, STAYING HOME AND PLAYING VIDEO-GAMES ALL DAY USED TO MAKE ME FEEL GUILTY...
BUT NOW WE CAN LITERALLY SAVE LIVES BY DOING JUST THAT...
PEER
I AM A MODEST, NOBLE HERO
CLOSE

MY PAL RACHEL WROTE A PUB QUIZ FOR A BUNCH OF US TO DO AT HOME OVER ZOOM...
QUESTION NUMBER 7...
ABOUT HALFWAY THROUGH THOUGH...
RUFUS DECIDED...
IT WAS ALL ABOUT HIM!

AFTER THE QUIZ I FELT A LITTLE DOWN IN THE DUMPS.

HEY

ARE YOU SAD BECAUSE YOU LOST THE QUIZ?

YOU ARE AN IDIOT AND YOUR FRIENDS ARE SUPER CLEVER. YOU MUST BE USED TO BEING INFERIOR TO THEM BY NOW.

I MISS BEING INFERIOR TO THEIR *FACES*... I USUALLY GET HUGS...

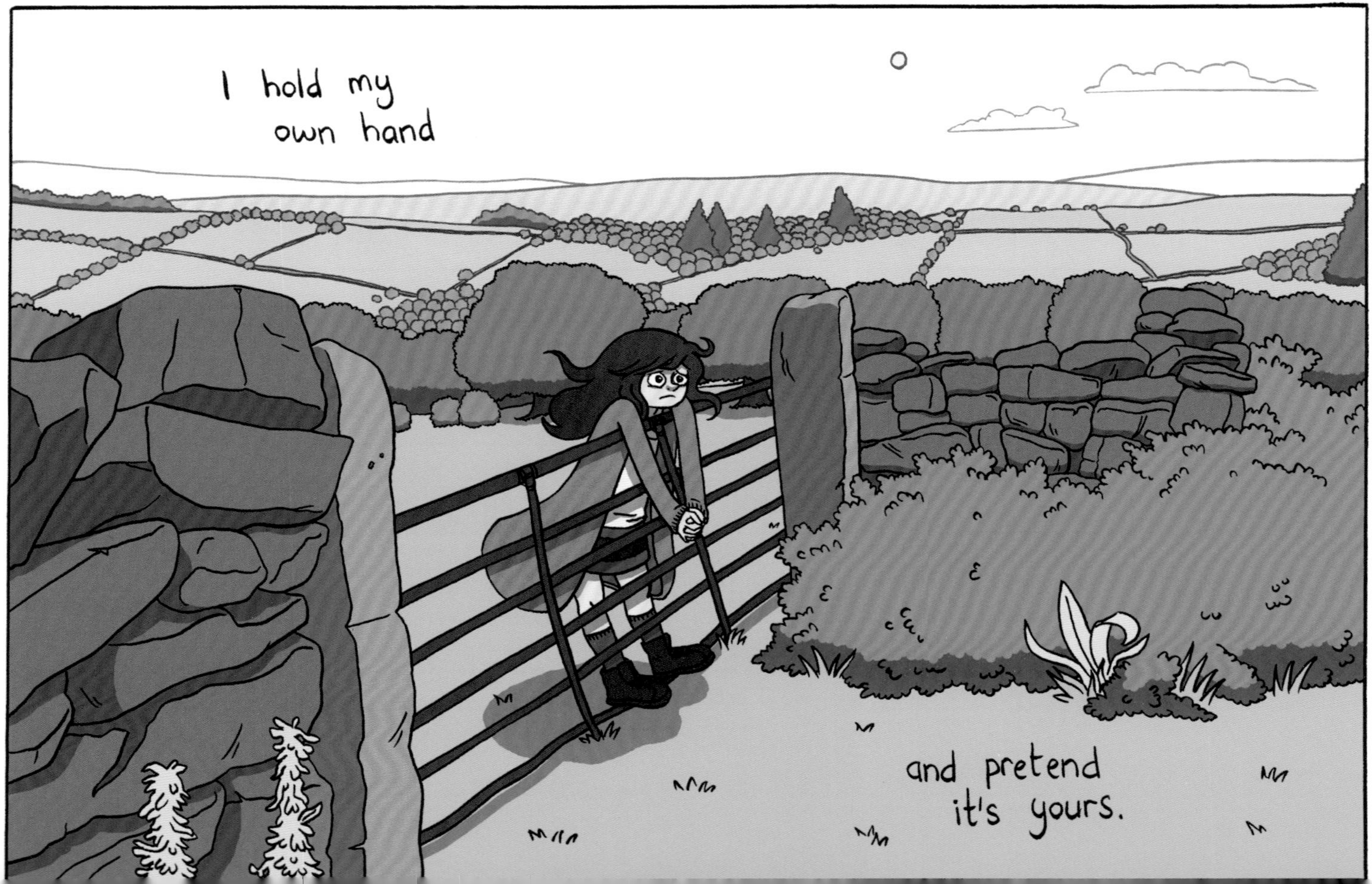
I hold my own hand
and pretend it's yours.

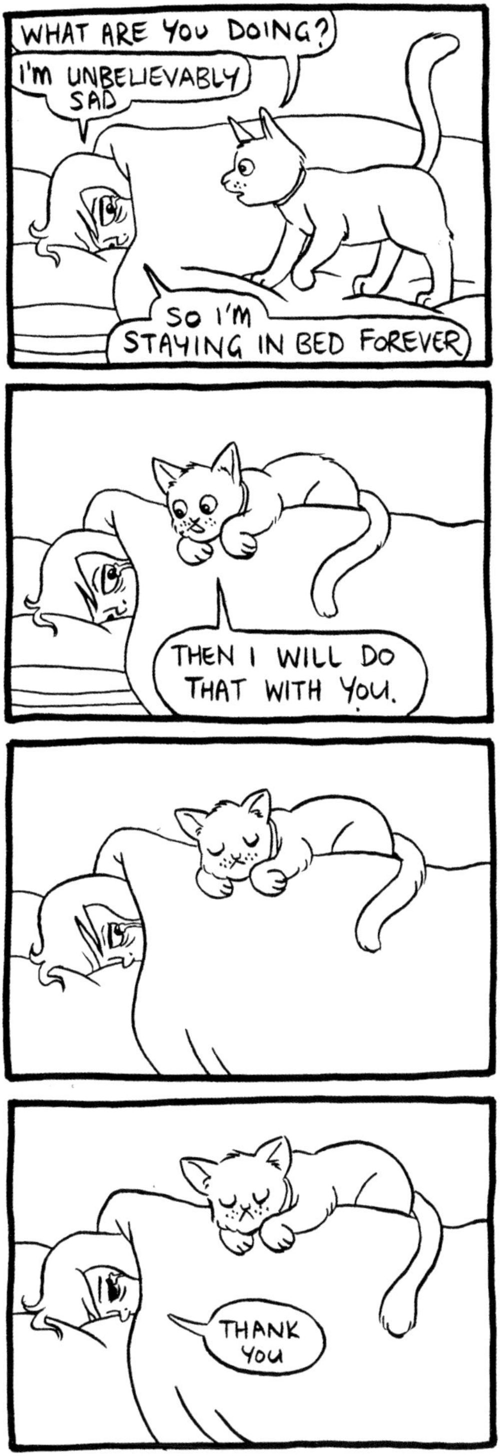
WHAT ARE YOU DOING?
I'M UNBELIEVABLY SAD
SO I'M STAYING IN BED FOREVER
THEN I WILL DO THAT WITH YOU.
THANK YOU

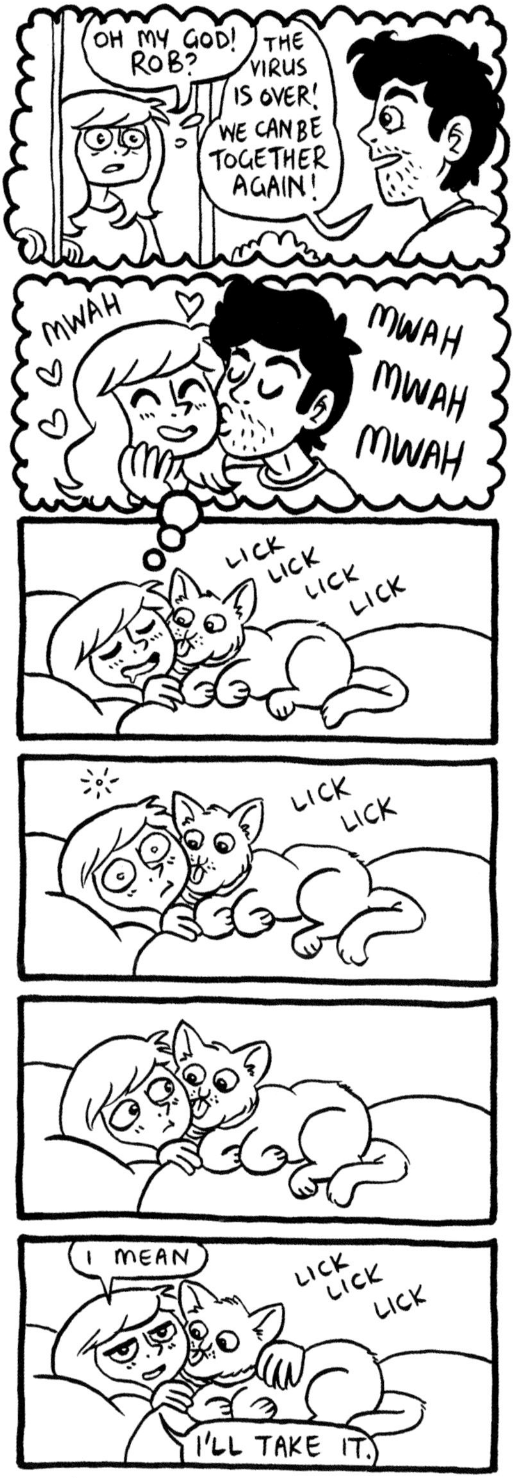
OH MY GOD! ROB?
THE VIRUS IS OVER! WE CAN BE TOGETHER AGAIN!
MWAH
MWAH MWAH MWAH
LICK LICK LICK LICK
LICK LICK
I MEAN
LICK LICK LICK
I'LL TAKE IT.

I ALWAYS THOUGHT THAT IF I EVER LIVED THROUGH A GLOBAL DISASTER IT WOULD FEEL LIKE BEING IN AN ACTION FILM...

EVERYONE! GET BEHIND ME! I WILL SACRIFICE MYSELF *VERY BRAVELY!!*

SO BRAVE...

EVERYONE! GET IN THIS VAN I CAN DEFINITELY DRIVE AND I WILL TAKE US TO SAFETY!!

WHAT A GREAT VAN!

SOMEHOW IT DIDN'T REALLY WORK OUT THAT WAY...

THANK YOU FOR PAYING OFF YOUR NOOK HOMES MORTGAGE!

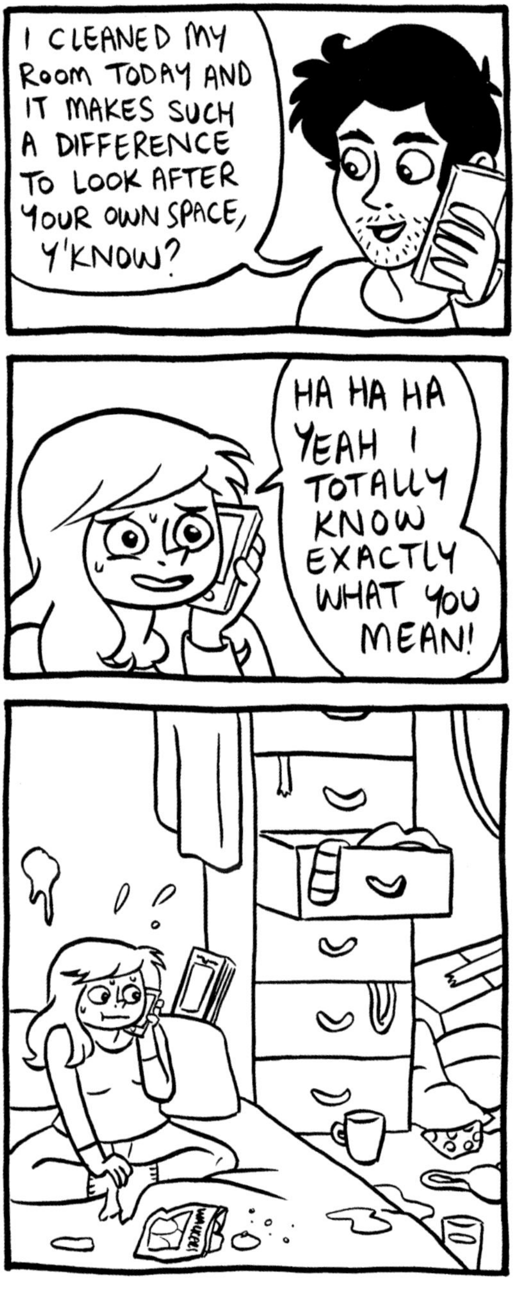
I CLEANED MY ROOM TODAY AND IT MAKES SUCH A DIFFERENCE TO LOOK AFTER YOUR OWN SPACE, Y'KNOW?
HA HA HA YEAH I TOTALLY KNOW EXACTLY WHAT YOU MEAN!

IT FEELS LIKE TIME IS ACTING REALLY STRANGELY IN THESE STRANGE TIMES...

HOW IS IT ALREADY 2PM?

WHY DOES APRIL HAVE 200 DAYS IN IT THIS YEAR??

HANG ON

WHAT HAPPENED TO WEDNESDAY?

BREAKFAST
BREAKFAST
MFF!
BREAKFAST
PUT
RUFUS
AT LEAST YOU GIVE ME A REASON TO GET OUT OF BED, EH, OLD FRIEND?
NOM NOM
RUFUS
I MEAN YOU CAN GO BACK TO BED NOW. I DON'T CARE.
RUFUS

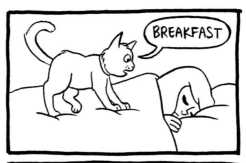

HOW TO MAKE THE PERFECT MATCHA LATTE!

1) mix a teaspoon of matcha powder with honey and warm water.

2) heat up some milk.

3) try not to think about how the world is ending.

4) mix together in your favourite mug.

5) enjoy!

mmm

SITTING IN MY GARDEN...
WITH A GLASS OF WINE AND THE SUN ON MY FACE...
I CAN ALMOST IMAGINE I'M ON HOLIDAY.
PEOPLE ARE DYING. STOP ENJOYING YOURSELF.
THAT'S BETTER

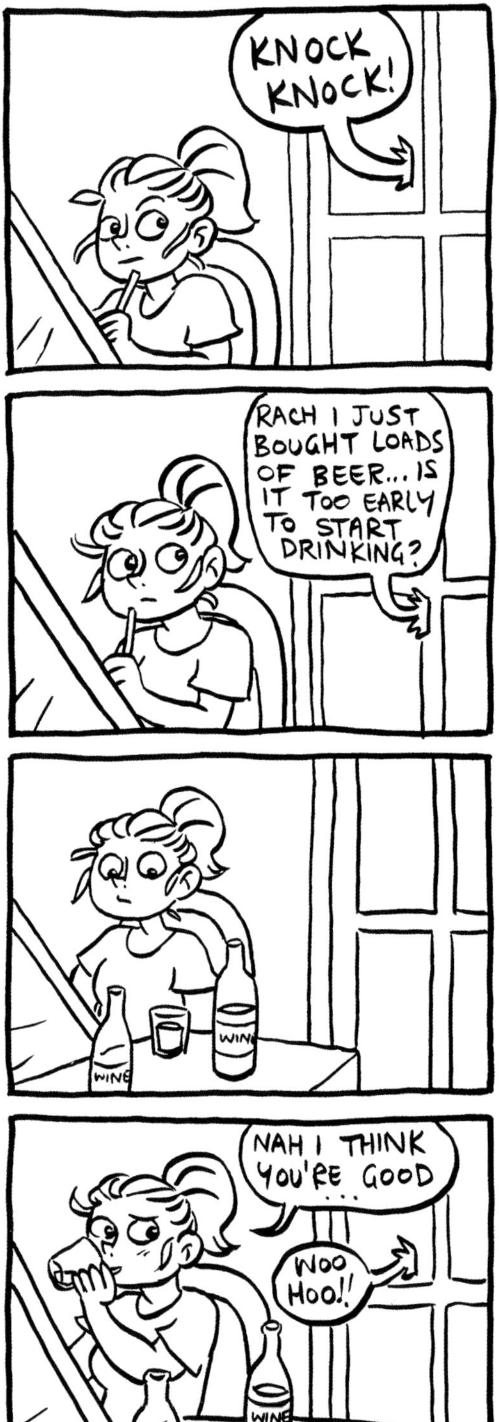
KNOCK KNOCK!
RACH I JUST BOUGHT LOADS OF BEER... IS IT TOO EARLY TO START DRINKING?
WINE
WINE
NAH I THINK YOU'RE GOOD ...
WOO HOO!!
WINE

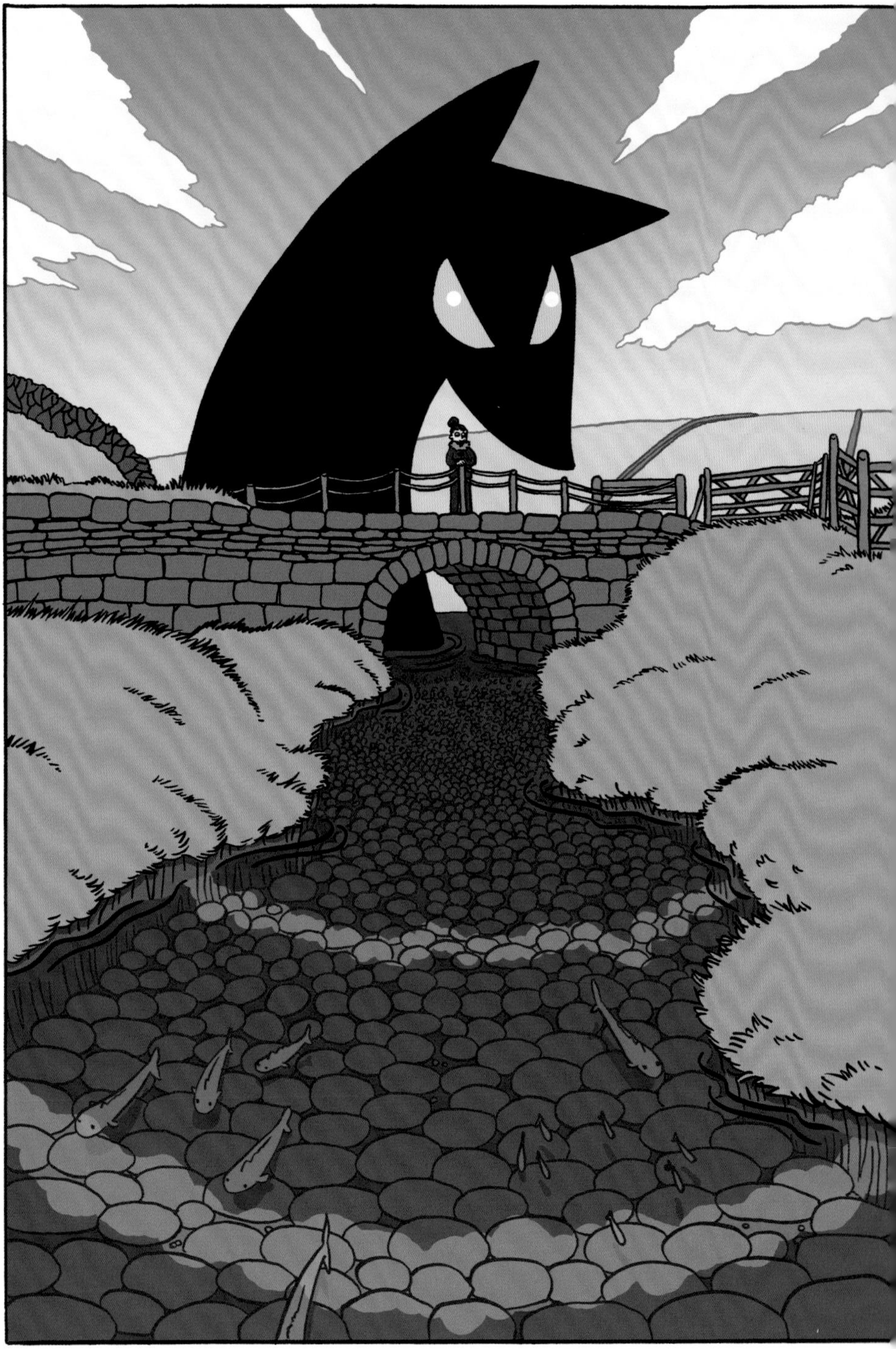

I ORDER 12 TUBS OF MY FAVOURITE INSTANT NOODLES ONLINE...
TAP TAP
I WATCH THE VAN MAKE ITS WAY TO ME VIA THE TRACKING INFO...
4 STOPS AWAY
3 STOPS AWAY
WHEN THEY ARRIVE I RIP INTO THE BOX IMMEDIATELY...
SNARL
I EAT TWO TUBS AT ONCE LIKE A GODDAMN FERAL RACCOON.
AM NAM NAM

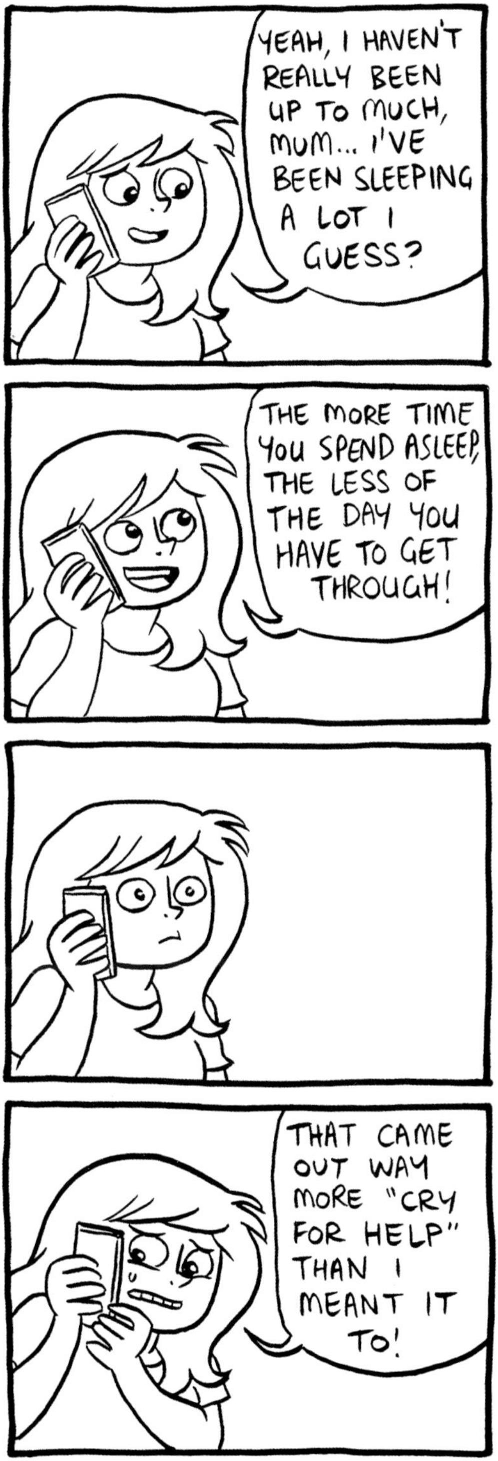
YEAH, I HAVEN'T REALLY BEEN UP TO MUCH, MUM... I'VE BEEN SLEEPING A LOT I GUESS?
THE MORE TIME YOU SPEND ASLEEP, THE LESS OF THE DAY YOU HAVE TO GET THROUGH!
THAT CAME OUT WAY MORE "CRY FOR HELP" THAN I MEANT IT TO!

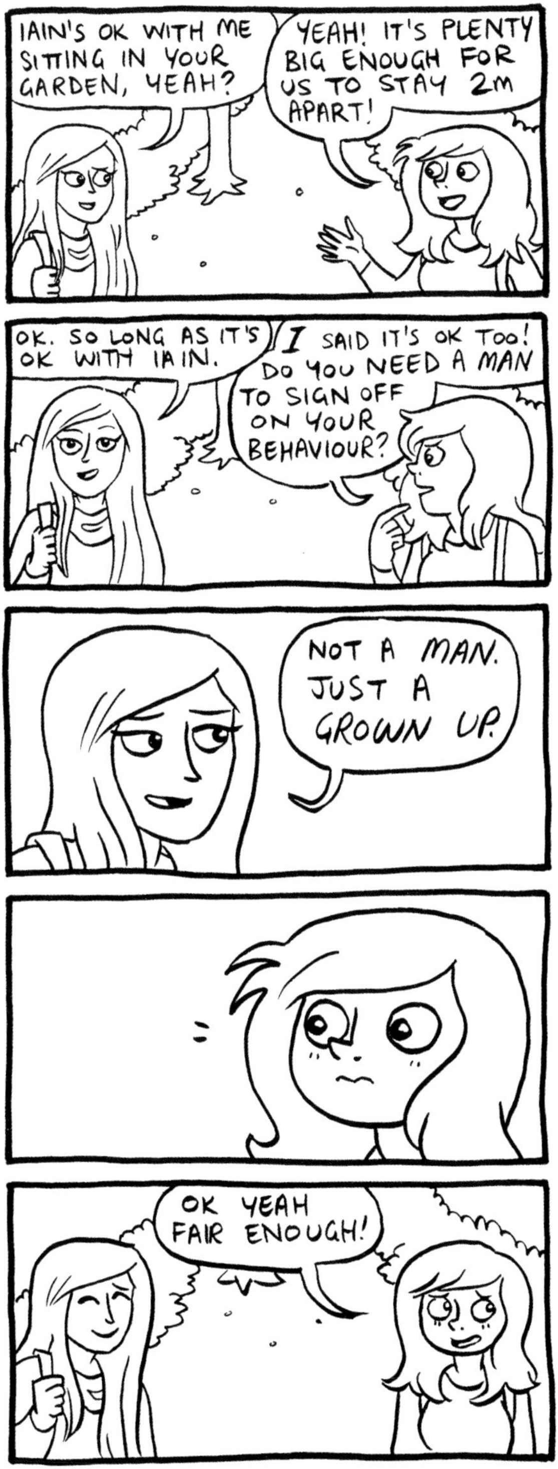
IAIN'S OK WITH ME SITTING IN YOUR GARDEN, YEAH?
YEAH! IT'S PLENTY BIG ENOUGH FOR US TO STAY 2m APART!
OK. SO LONG AS IT'S OK WITH IAIN.
I SAID IT'S OK TOO! DO YOU NEED A MAN TO SIGN OFF ON YOUR BEHAVIOUR?
NOT A MAN. JUST A GROWN UP.
OK YEAH FAIR ENOUGH!

I MISS ROB
ABSENCE MAKES THE HEART GROW FONDER
NO BUT LISTEN...
MY ABSENCE AND MY FONDNESS METERS ARE FULL ALREADY!
ABSENCE
FONDNESS
TAP TAP
I'M MAXED OUT ON BOTH THINGS IN THAT IDIOM!
I DUNNO THEN. JUST BE LESS OF A NERD I GUESS.

PEOPLE AT MY LOCAL SUPER--MARKET ARE USUALLY REALLY SENSIBLE... THERE'S ONE REALLY ANNOYING LADY WHO I KEEP LITERALLY BUMP--ING INTO THOUGH... LUCKILY I'VE FOUND A GOOD WAY OF PUTTING HER OFF OF TOUCHING ME.
SHOVE
DON'T WORRY! I'M NOT CONTAGIOUS!
I AM
SCARPER
HEH HEH

THERE ARE SO MANY WAYS TO KEEP IN TOUCH RIGHT NOW. SO MANY WAYS TO TALK TO PEOPLE.
BUT BECAUSE I'M NOT DOING ANYTHING... I FEEL I HAVE NOTHING INTERESTING TO SAY.
I MISS COMFORTABLE SILENCES.

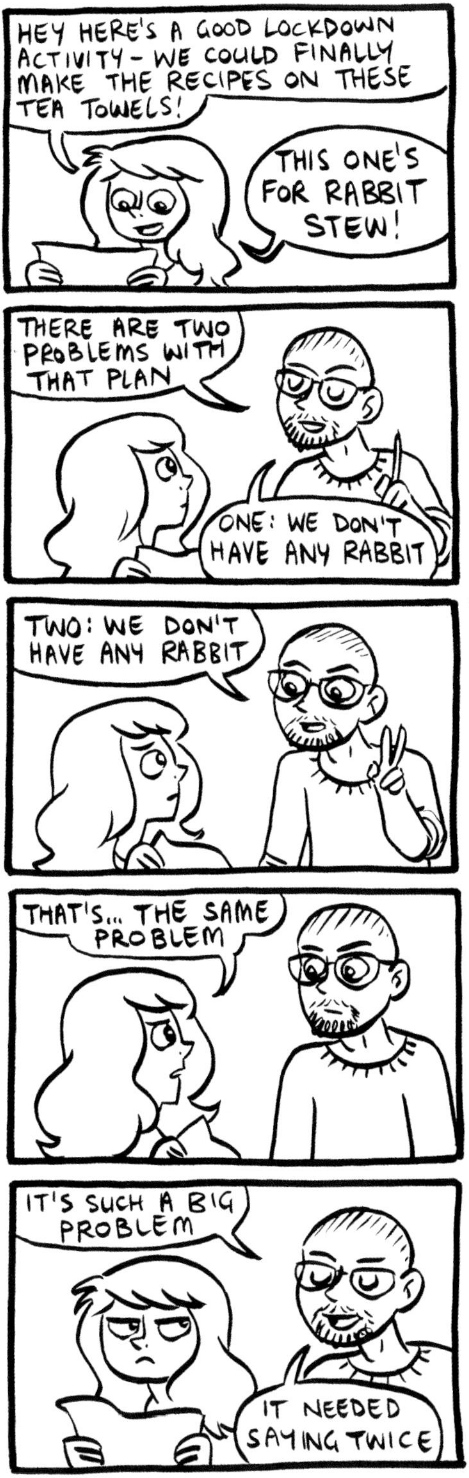
HEY HERE'S A GOOD LOCKDOWN ACTIVITY - WE COULD FINALLY MAKE THE RECIPES ON THESE TEA TOWELS!
THIS ONE'S FOR RABBIT STEW!
THERE ARE TWO PROBLEMS WITH THAT PLAN
ONE: WE DON'T HAVE ANY RABBIT
TWO: WE DON'T HAVE ANY RABBIT
THAT'S... THE SAME PROBLEM
IT'S SUCH A BIG PROBLEM
IT NEEDED SAYING TWICE

AH LITTLE BEE! YOU DON'T KNOW WHAT'S GOING ON, DO YOU?
ALL OUR HUMAN STRESSES MEAN NOTHING TO YOU... YOU JUST GET TO HANG WITH YOUR PALS AND MAKE YOUR HONEY...
I'VE BEEN COLLECTING POLLEN FOR 8 HOURS TODAY. YOU GOT UP AT 11 AND STARTED DRINKING AT 12.
BUT YEAH... I'M SORRY ABOUT YOUR STRESSFUL LIFE I GUESS

I MISS
BEING
GHOST STORIES
CLOSE
TO YOU.

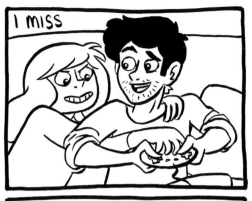

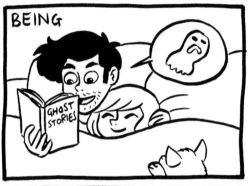

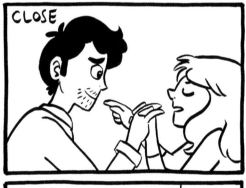

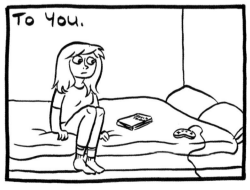

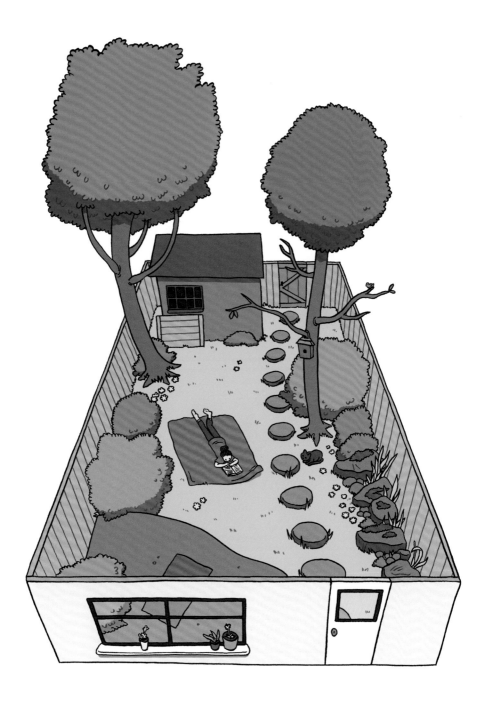

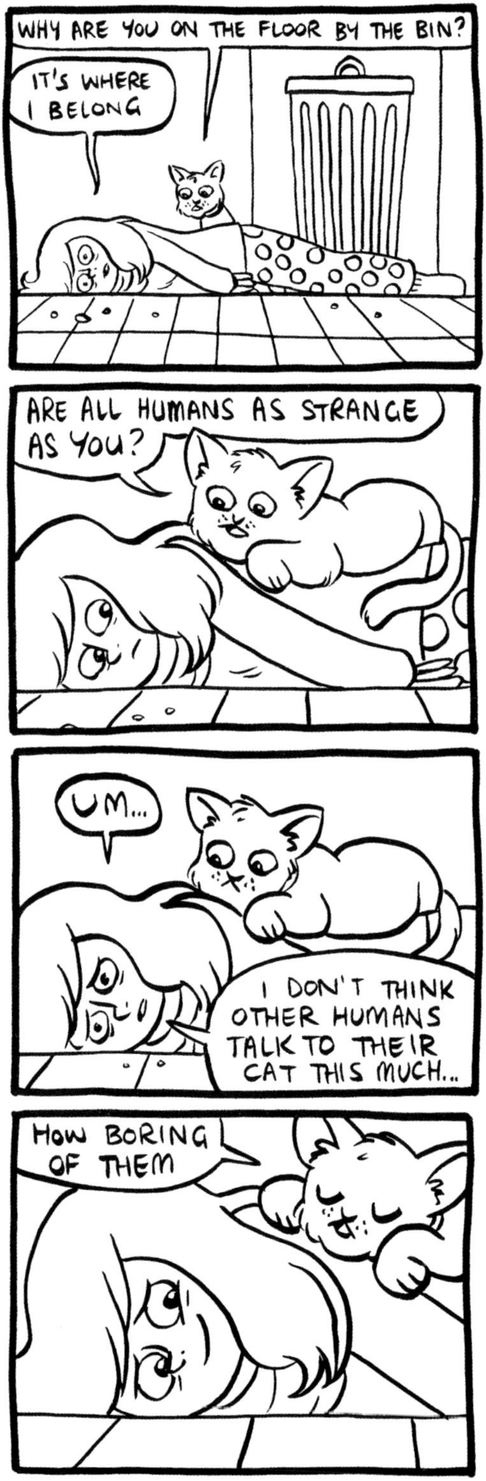
WHY ARE YOU ON THE FLOOR BY THE BIN?
IT'S WHERE I BELONG
ARE ALL HUMANS AS STRANGE AS YOU?
UM...
I DON'T THINK OTHER HUMANS TALK TO THEIR CAT THIS MUCH...
HOW BORING OF THEM

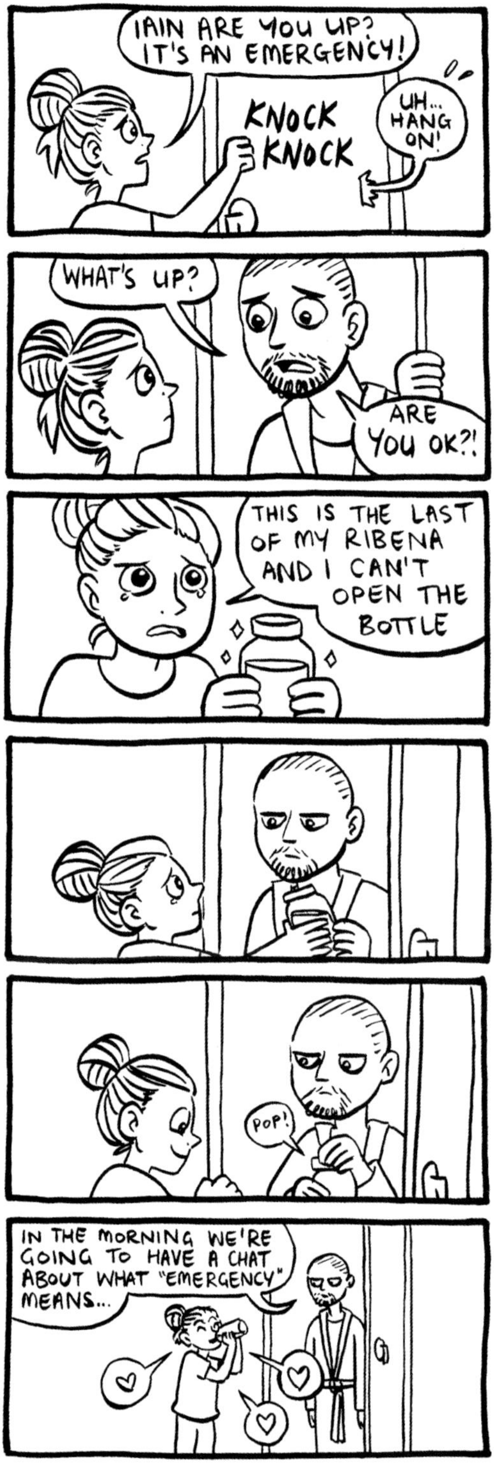
IAIN ARE YOU UP? IT'S AN EMERGENCY!
KNOCK KNOCK
UH... HANG ON!
WHAT'S UP?
ARE YOU OK?!
THIS IS THE LAST OF MY RIBENA AND I CAN'T OPEN THE BOTTLE
POP!
IN THE MORNING WE'RE GOING TO HAVE A CHAT ABOUT WHAT "EMERGENCY" MEANS...

I HAD A HUGE MENTAL HEALTH FLARE UP THE OTHER NIGHT AND POSTED SOME STUPID STUFF ON SOCIAL MEDIA
TWEET
05:23
Draft
Cancel
What is the fucking point in me
I CHECKED MY PHONE IN THE MORNING...
AND THERE WAS AN OUTPOURING OF LOVE AND UNDERSTANDING AND CONCERN. EVEN FROM FOLK WHO HAD NEVER MET ME.
I HAVE TO KEEP GOING.

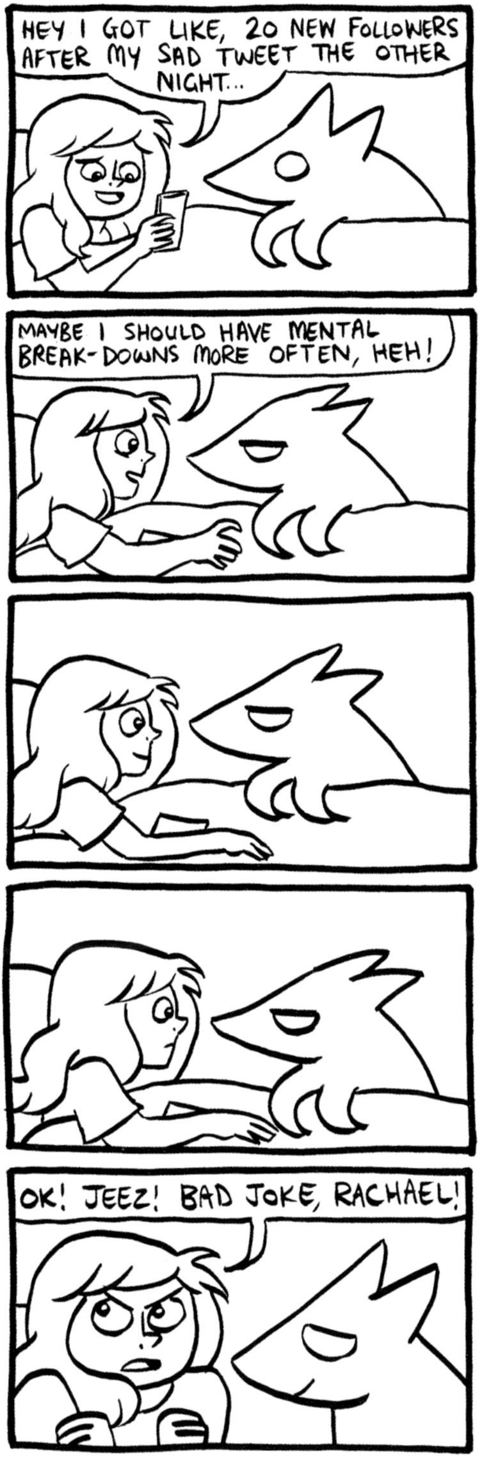
HEY I GOT LIKE, 20 NEW FOLLOWERS AFTER MY SAD TWEET THE OTHER NIGHT...
MAYBE I SHOULD HAVE MENTAL BREAK-DOWNS MORE OFTEN, HEH!
OK! JEEZ! BAD JOKE, RACHAEL!

I WATCH ROB OPEN HIS BIRTHDAY PRESENTS FROM ME OVER ZOOM
OH WOW COOL!
I WISH SO BAD THAT I COULD BE THERE WITH HIM, BUT IT'S SO NICE TO SEE HIS FACE
GONNA SMOOCH THE HECKING HECK OUTA THAT FACE WHEN I'M ALLOWED
THERE IS A VERY REAL RISK OF ME KILLING MY BOYFRIEND WITH SMOOCHES WHEN THIS IS OVER...
OH I'VE WANTED THIS ONE FOR AGES!
HAHA YAYY

SINCE THE LOCKDOWN I'VE BEEN GROWING OUT MY HAIR AND REALLY TRYING TO LOOK AFTER IT.
100 STROKES
AS A RESULT IT LOOKS SUPER HEALTHY AND SHINY! ALL MY PALS ARE GONNA NOTICE WHEN WE'RE FINALLY ABLE TO HANG OUT!
IT'LL HOPEFULLY DISTRACT THEM FROM THE 20 POUNDS I'M DEFS GOING TO HAVE PUT ON.

OH! MY DARLING ROB... I WONDER IF YOU ARE LOOKING AT THE MOON TOO...?
YOU COULD TEXT HIM?
WHEN WILL I SEE YOUR FACE AGAIN...?
MY LOVE
MY OWN
YOU COULD JUST SKYPE HIM?
SHUSH! I'M BEING DRAMATIC AND TRAGIC LIKE I'M IN A ROMANTIC NOVEL!
YOU LITERALLY HAVE A ZOOM QUIZ NIGHT DATE WITH HIM IN FIFTEEN MINUTES...
IT'S HARD BEING TRAGIC WHEN YOU LIVE IN THE FUTURE

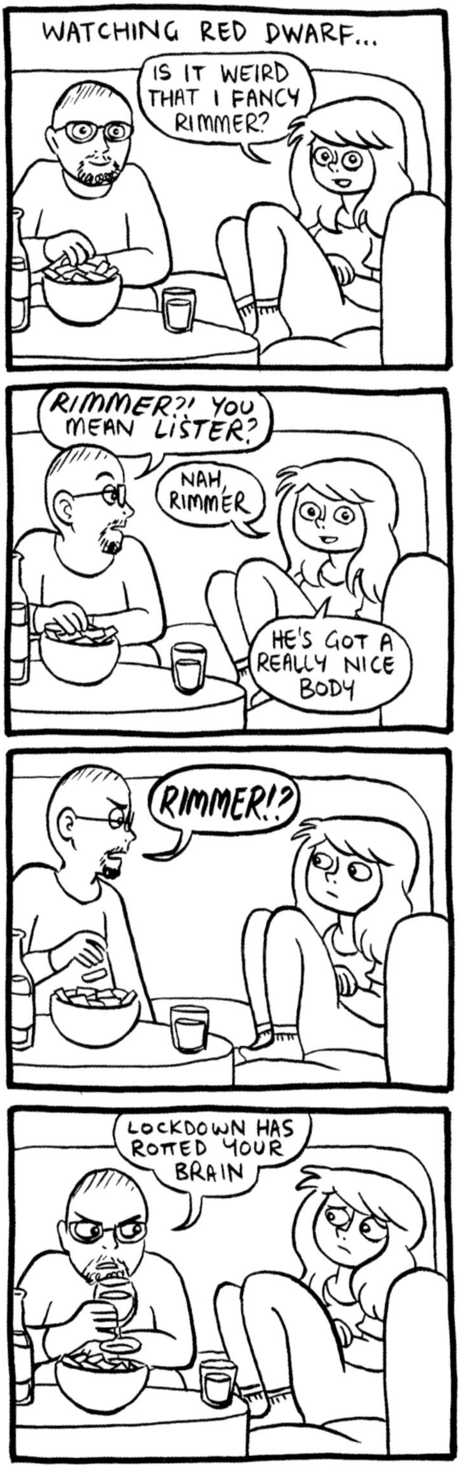
WATCHING RED DWARF...
IS IT WEIRD THAT I FANCY RIMMER?
RIMMER?! YOU MEAN LISTER?
NAH, RIMMER
HE'S GOT A REALLY NICE BODY
RIMMER!?
LOCKDOWN HAS ROTTED YOUR BRAIN

I WEAR MY NEW MASK FOR THE FIRST TIME
I FEEL PROTECTED!
TEENS
WILLIAM MORRIS PRINT
"LOOK AT ME! I'M A PARANOID IDIOT!"
HA HA HA HA!
I GUESS MASKS DON'T PROTECT FROM STUPID MEANIES...

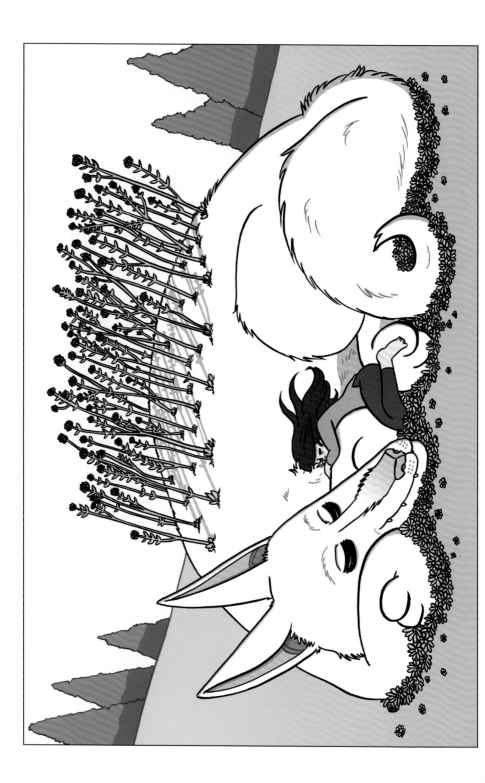

I FEEL BAD THAT WE HAVE PALS ROUND TO OUR GARDEN... SHOULD WE STOP DOING THAT? WE ONLY HAVE ONE PAL AT A TIME...
UGH!
STEBBEN
HEATHER
I HATE HOW WE HAVE TO JUSTIFY EVERYTHING THESE DAYS...
I DIDN'T REALISE THE APOCALYPSE WAS GOING TO BE SO JUDGEMENTAL!
OK THAT IS LITERALLY MY FAVOURITE THING ANYONE HAS SAID SO FAR ABOUT THIS SITUATION

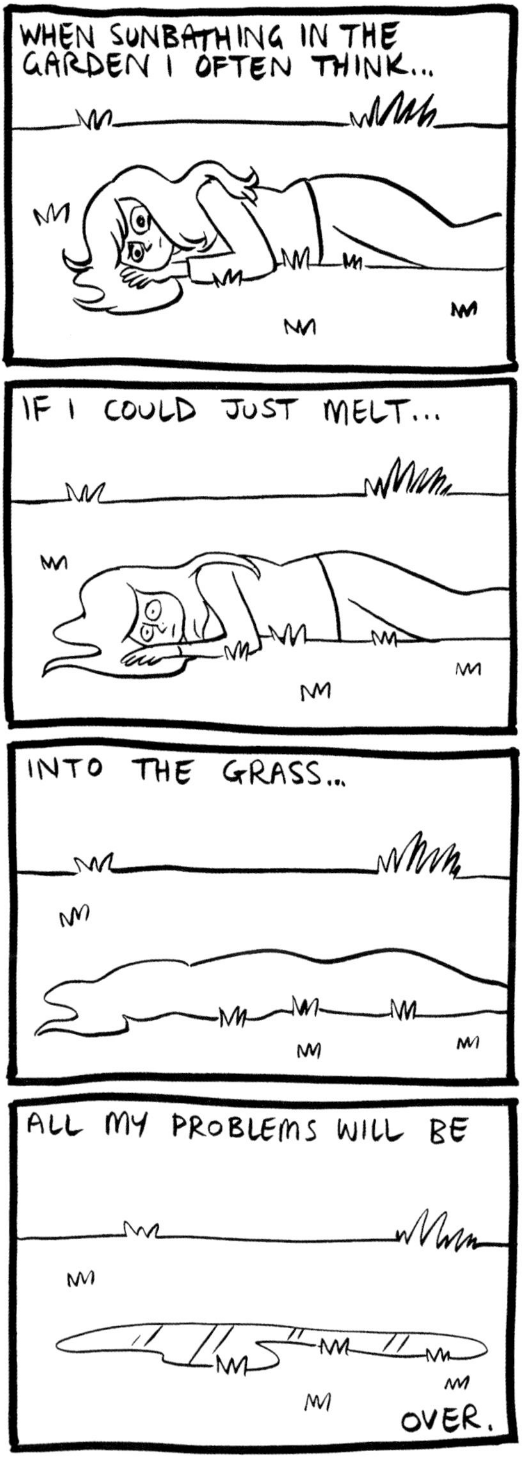
WHEN SUNBATHING IN THE GARDEN I OFTEN THINK...
IF I COULD JUST MELT...
INTO THE GRASS...
ALL MY PROBLEMS WILL BE
OVER.

I GO ON THE SAME WALK AS A COUPLE OF WEEKS BACK TO SEE THE LAMBS AGAIN.

THEY HAD GOTTEN SO BIG! THEY WERE NOW MUCH MORE CONFIDENT, CHARGING ABOUT LIKE THEY OWNED THE PLACE

MAAA

IT GAVE ME HOPE.

MAA

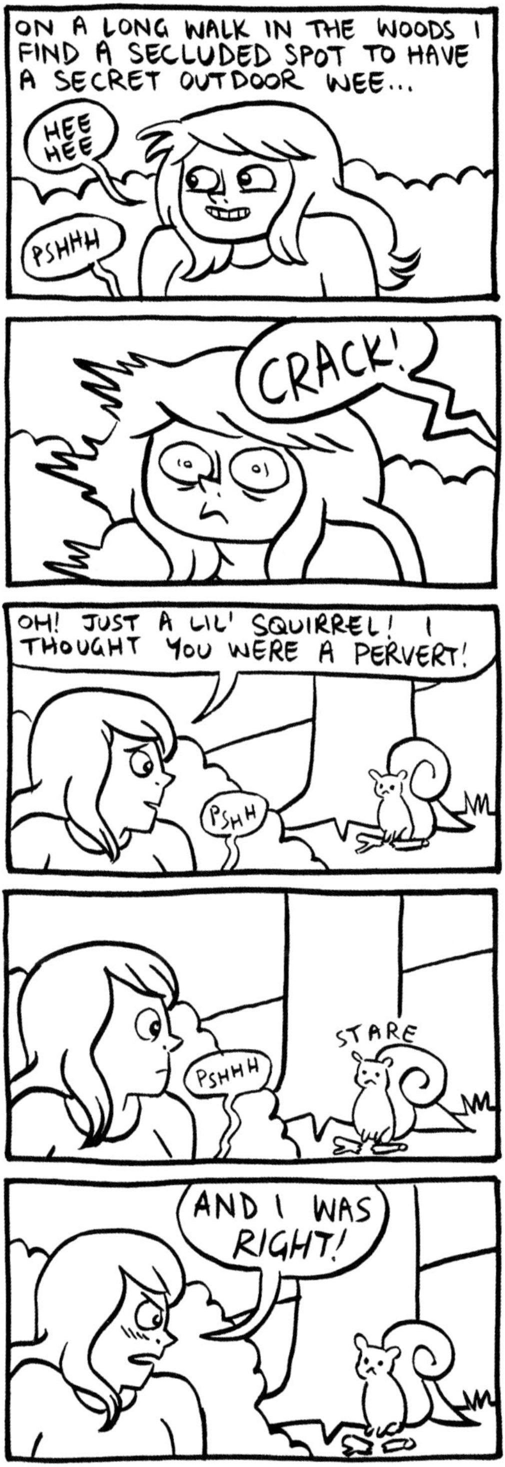
ON A LONG WALK IN THE WOODS I FIND A SECLUDED SPOT TO HAVE A SECRET OUTDOOR WEE...
HEE HEE
PSHHH
CRACK!
OH! JUST A LIL' SQUIRREL! I THOUGHT YOU WERE A PERVERT!
PSHH
STARE
PSHHH
AND I WAS RIGHT!

OK, YOUR ORDER WILL BE WITH YOU IN 30 MINUTES ...WAS THERE ANYTHING ELSE?
YEAH!!
ARE YOU ON TWITTER?
WHAT'S YOUR FAVOURITE COLOUR?
DID YOU SEE ENDGAME?
MA'AM, WE'RE VERY BUSY IN THIS TAKEAWAY RIGHT NOW-
I KNOW BUT...
IT'S BEEN SO LONG SINCE I MADE A NEW FRIEND!
I'M HANGING UP NOW...

JENI CAME OVER TO THE GARDEN TO DO SOME SOCIALLY-DISTANCED EMBROIDERY!
SO IF YOU WANTED TO HAVE A GO, RACH, YOU COULD MAYBE EMBROIDER ONE OF YOUR COMICS!
HMM...
KNOWS NOTHING ABOUT SEWING
MAYBE I COULD START WITH LIKE... A BLOB?
ALSO GOOD!

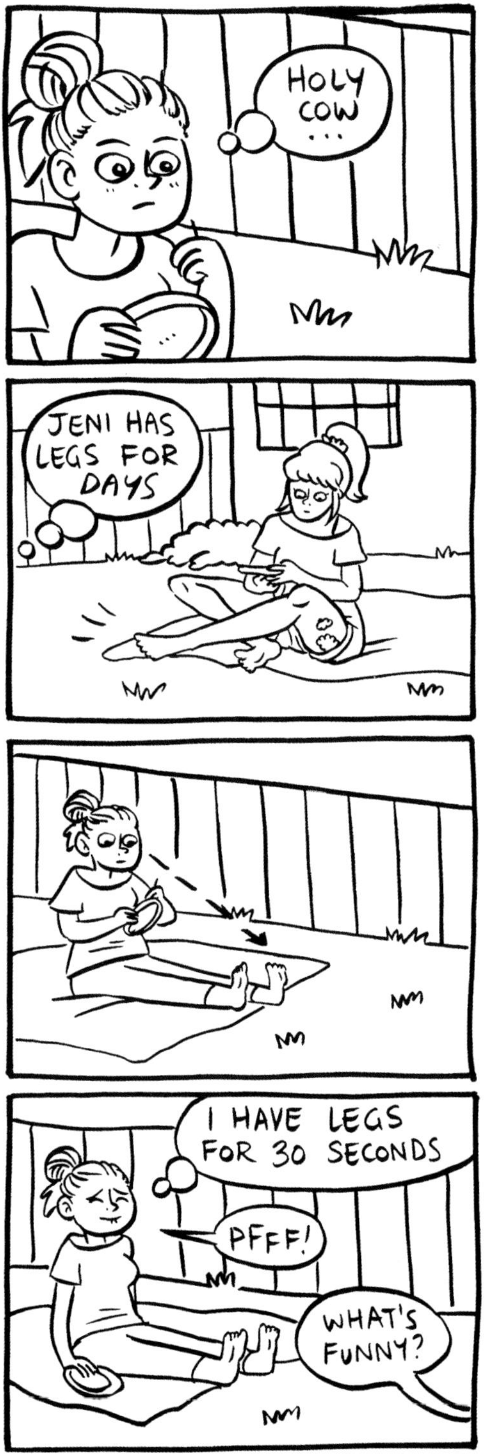

HOLY COW ...
JENI HAS LEGS FOR DAYS
I HAVE LEGS FOR 30 SECONDS
PFFF!
WHAT'S FUNNY?

I'M VERY GRATEFUL TO HAVE MY BACK GARDEN. I'VE BEEN SPENDING A LOT OF TIME IN IT LATELY.

I LIKE WATCHING THE BEES EXPLORE THE DIFFERENT FLOWERS.

I KNOW THEY'RE TECHNICALLY WEEDS BUT I LIKE THE DANDELIONS BEST. THEY'RE SO ROUND AND FUZZY.

LIKE NATURE'S POM POMS!

OH GOD, IT'S THAT MAN WHO ALWAYS YELLS CREEPY SHIT AT ME...
ALRIGHT LOVE! WE'LL GET THROUGH THIS, EH?!
AW... MAYBE THIS HAS BROUGHT OUT THE GOOD IN HIM!
BET YOU'VE STOPPED WEARING BRAS, EH?!
AAAAAND THERE IT IS

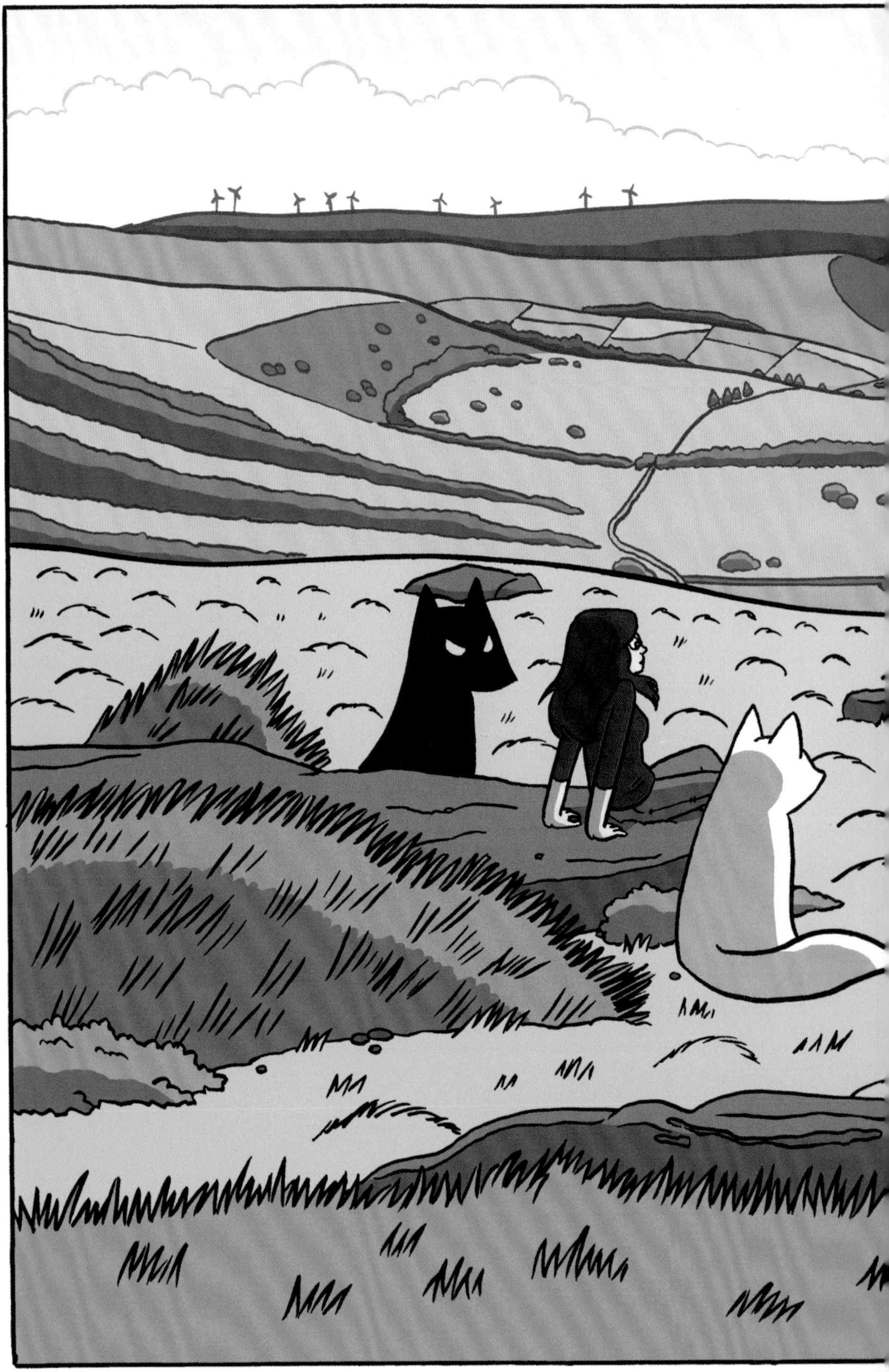

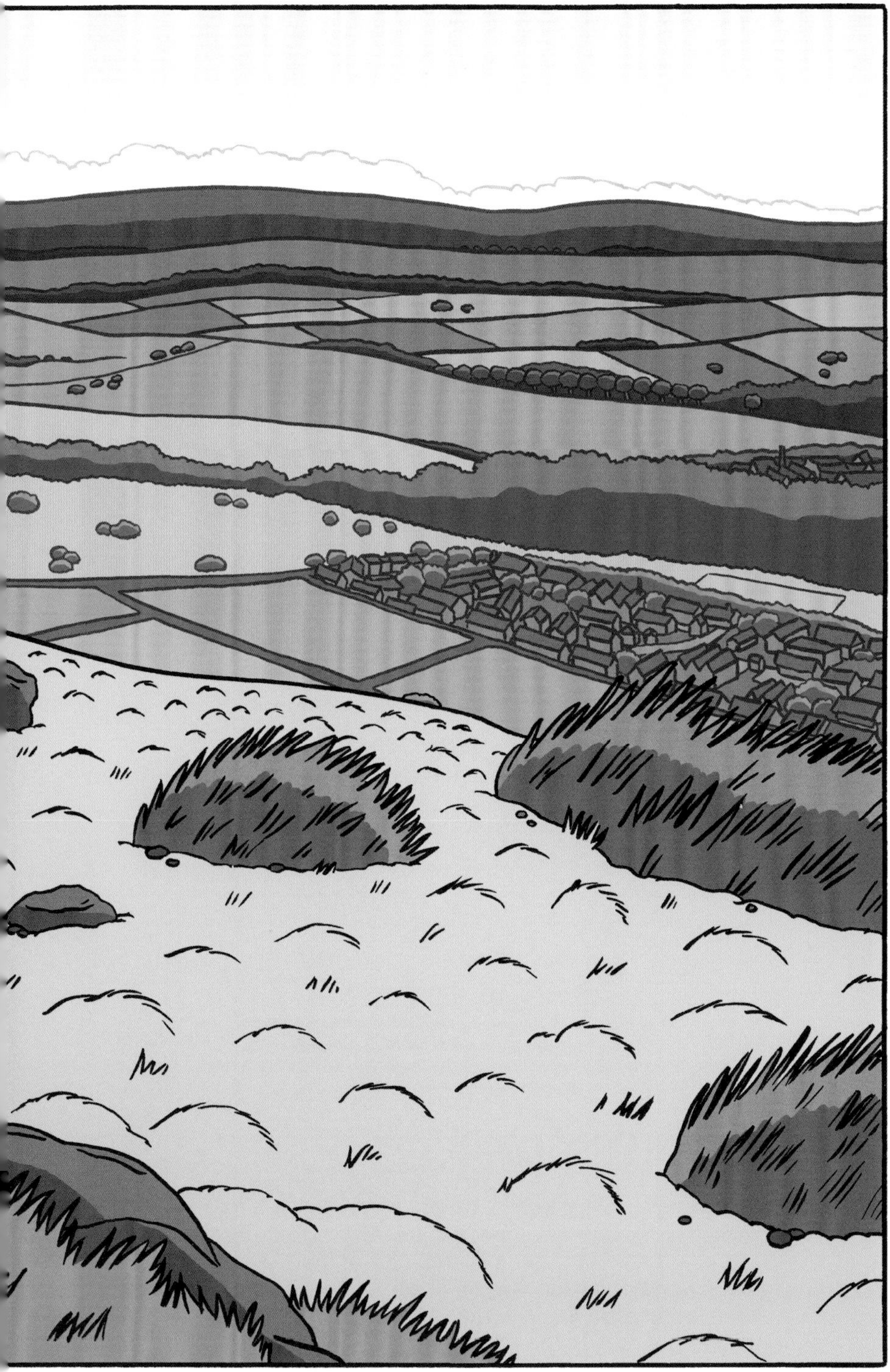

HEY WHAT ARE YOUR PLANS TODAY?
← IAIN MAKING BREAKFAST
WELL... I CAN'T REMEMBER WHEN I LAST HAD A BATH...
SOOOO
I SHOULD PROBS DO THAT...
YYEAH...

IF ALL YOU ARE DOING

RIGHT NOW

IS SURVIVING

THAT IS FINE.

I GO ON A DANGEROUS TRIP TO THE SHOP...
BURGER BUNS AND KITCHEN FOIL... BURGER BUNS AND KITCHEN FOIL...
20 MINUTES LATER...
SO... I DIDN'T DO TOO GOOD... I COULD ONLY GET WHOLEMEAL BUNS
AND THEY DIDN'T HAVE KITCHEN FOIL SO I GOT... BAKING PARCHMENT?
UH... RIGHT... I HATE WHOLEMEAL BUNS... AND I ACTUALLY ASKED YOU FOR KITCHEN ROLL...
WOW. I DID MUCH WORSE THAN I THOUGHT I HAD...
IT'S OK!

I'VE BEEN PRINTING MASKS THIS MORNING AND-
BOY HOOMAN!
OH! HEY RUFUS!
BOY HOOMAN IS IN A BOX!!
RUFUS GET OFF THE SCREEN!
WHY IS BOY HOOMAN IN A BOX!?
WOW HE'S VERY MEOW-Y TODAY!
YEAH I DUNNO WHY!
I WILL SAVE YOU BOY HOOMAN!!

I SOMETIMES PRETEND THAT SOCIAL DISTANCING IS A VIDEO GAME...
HP
ENERGY
MINI BOSS: GUY WHO JUST STOMPS TOWARDS YOU SO YOU HAVE TO JUMP OUT OF HIS WAY...
STOMP
STOMP
STOMP
MINI BOSS: PAIR OF JOGGERS WHO GO EITHER SIDE OF YOU...
YIKES!
THERE'S ALWAYS A FINAL BOSS THAT I'M NOT READY FOR...
FINAL BOSS: A FAMILY OF SEVEN.
THAT'S ENOUGH OUTDOORS TIME FOR TODAY!!

FOR A WHILE NOW I'VE BEEN TRYING TO RECONNECT WITH AN OLD FRIEND...

BUT IT'S RESULTED IN A STRING OF UNANSWERED TEXTS AND CALLS...

YOU'VE REACHED THE VOICE-MAIL OF ...

PEOPLE DRIFT APART AND I GET THAT... BUT I REALLY VALUED THIS FRIENDSHIP.

YOU SHOULD TAKE A HINT, RACHAEL

TURN

I MEAN... YEAH MAYBE YOU SHOULD TAKE A HINT...

OH COME ON!

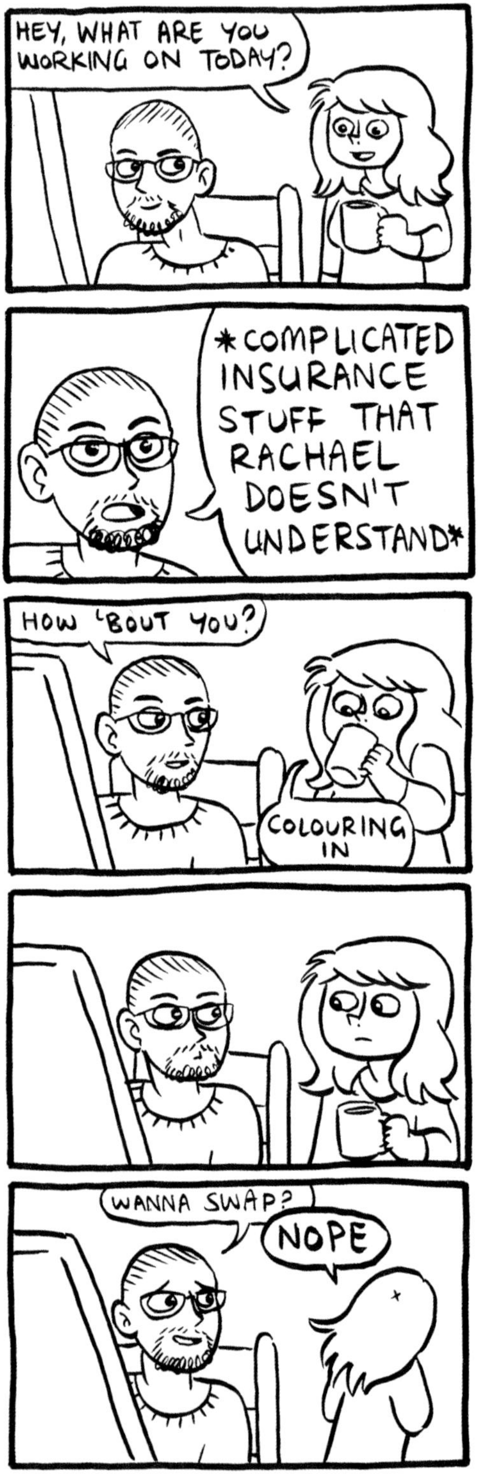
HEY, WHAT ARE YOU WORKING ON TODAY?
COMPLICATED INSURANCE STUFF THAT RACHAEL DOESN'T UNDERSTAND
HOW 'BOUT YOU?
COLOURING IN
WANNA SWAP?
NOPE

IT BREAKS MY HEART THAT WE CAN'T BE TOGETHER RIGHT NOW.
BUT I NEED YOU TO KNOW...
YOU'RE MAKING THIS EASIER...
JUST BY EXISTING.

I HAVE A PLANT IN MY ROOM HANGING FROM MY SKYLIGHT...
LATELY IT'S HAD A BIG GROWTH SPURT!
IT'S ALMOST TOUCHING THE FLOOR!
SNIF SNIF
MAYBE BY THE TIME IT DOES... ALL THIS WILL BE OVER.

TIME HAS NO MEANING ANYMORE
ALL THE DAYS ARE MERGING INTO ONE
THEREFORE WE ARE FREE TO DO WHAT WE LIKE *WHEN* WE LIKE
FOR THE *LAST* TIME! IT'S 2AM! I'M *NOT* GIVING YOU YOUR BREAKFAST!!
RATS

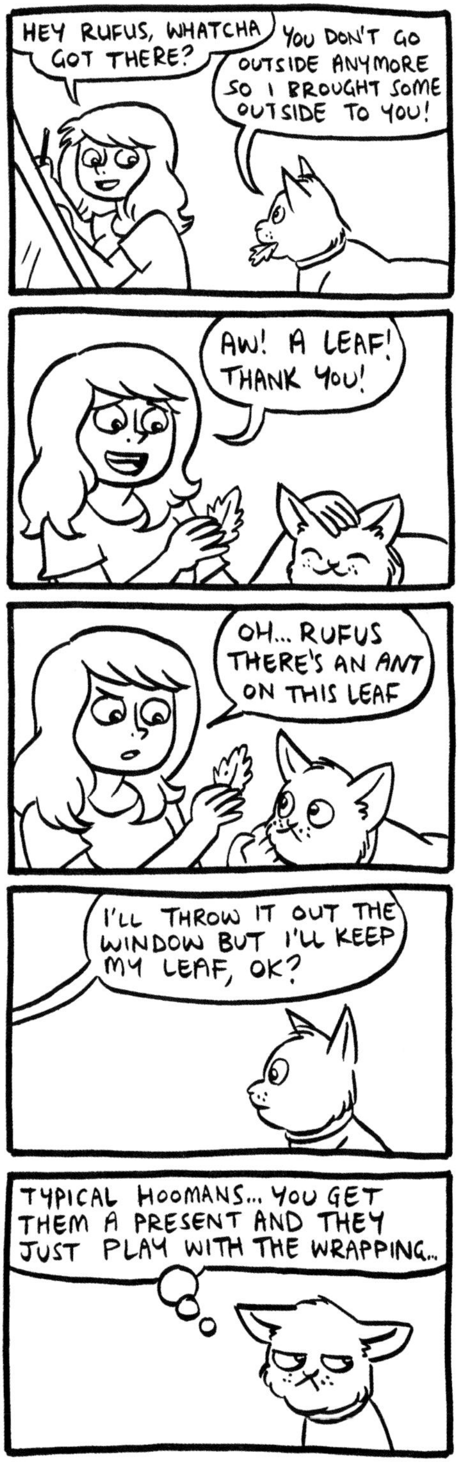
HEY RUFUS, WHATCHA GOT THERE?
YOU DON'T GO OUTSIDE ANYMORE SO I BROUGHT SOME OUTSIDE TO YOU!
AW! A LEAF! THANK YOU!
OH... RUFUS THERE'S AN ANT ON THIS LEAF
I'LL THROW IT OUT THE WINDOW BUT I'LL KEEP MY LEAF, OK?
TYPICAL HOOMANS... YOU GET THEM A PRESENT AND THEY JUST PLAY WITH THE WRAPPING...

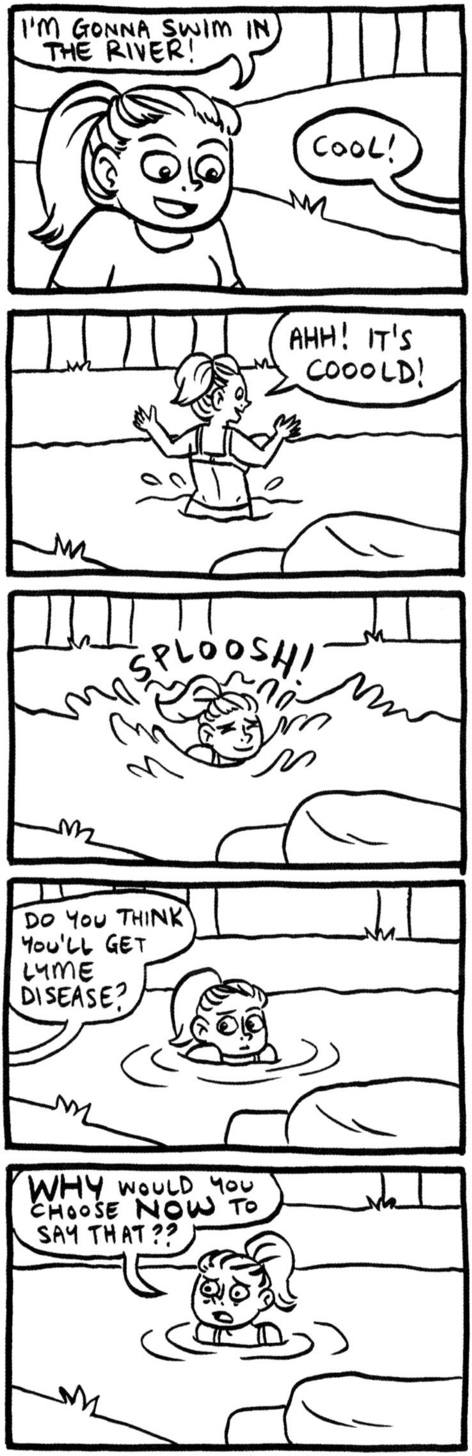
I'M GONNA SWIM IN THE RIVER!
COOL!
AHH! IT'S COOOLD!
SPLOOSH!
DO YOU THINK YOU'LL GET LYME DISEASE?
WHY WOULD YOU CHOOSE NOW TO SAY THAT??

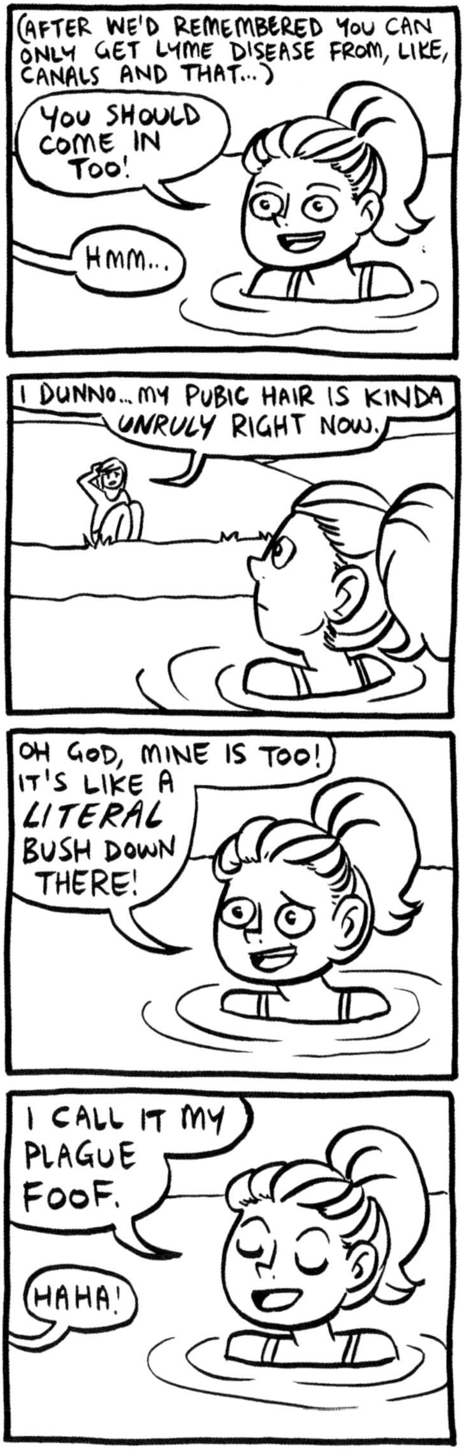
(AFTER WE'D REMEMBERED YOU CAN ONLY GET LYME DISEASE FROM, LIKE, CANALS AND THAT...)
YOU SHOULD COME IN TOO!
HMM...
I DUNNO... MY PUBIC HAIR IS KINDA *UNRULY* RIGHT NOW.
OH GOD, MINE IS TOO! IT'S LIKE A *LITERAL* BUSH DOWN THERE!
I CALL IT MY PLAGUE FOOF.
HAHA!

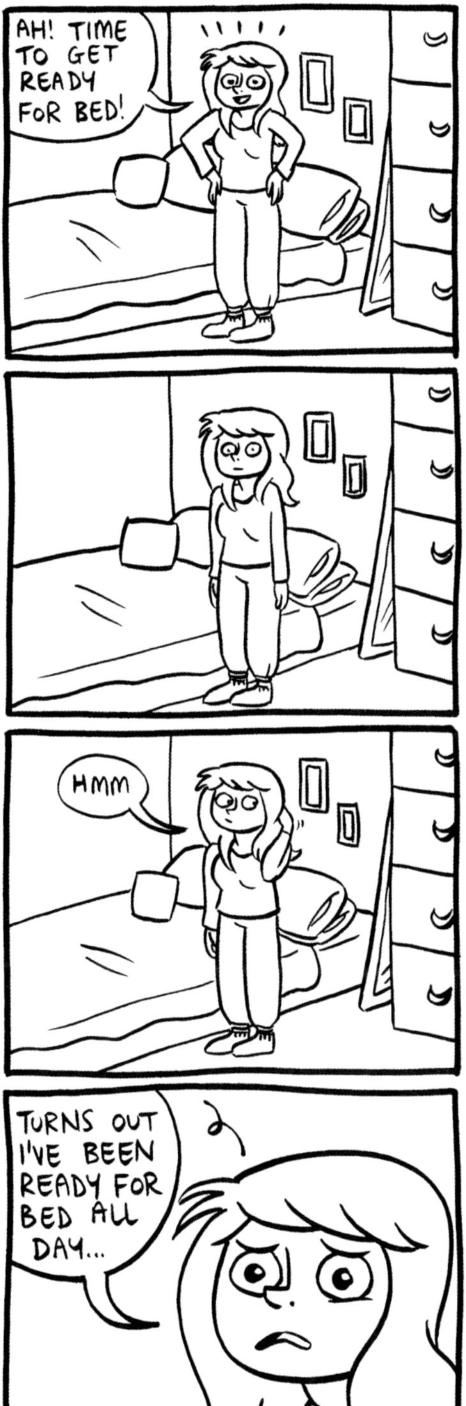
AH! TIME TO GET READY FOR BED!
HMM
TURNS OUT I'VE BEEN READY FOR BED ALL DAY...

SIGH
YOU LOOK LIKE SHIT
I KNOW!
YOU LOOK LIKE SHIT
DON'T YOU START!

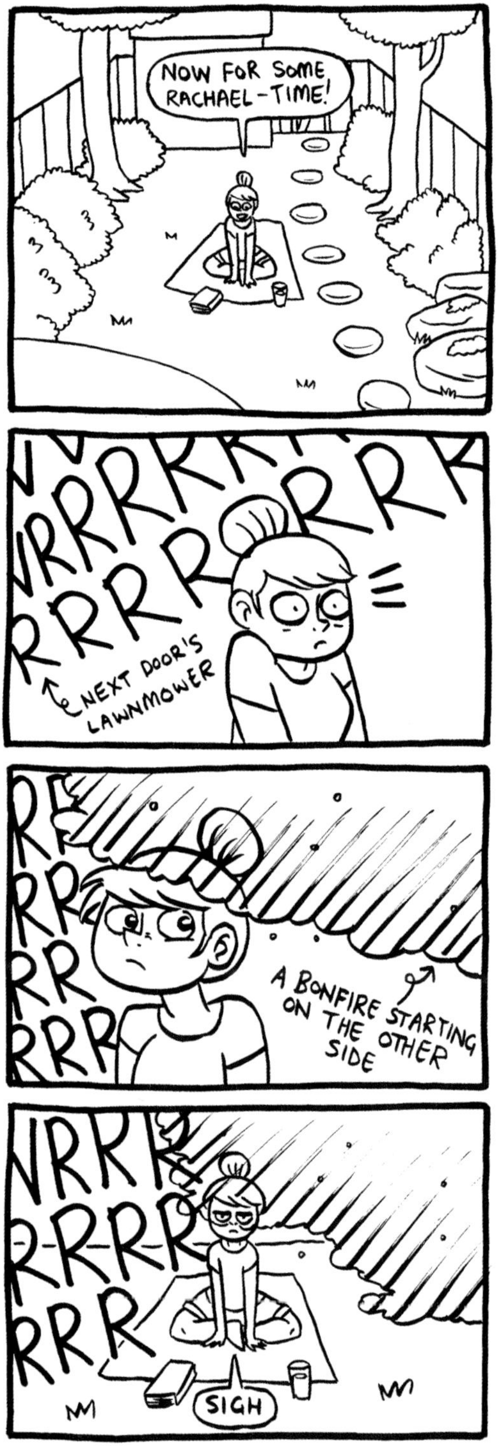
NOW FOR SOME RACHAEL-TIME!
NEXT DOOR'S LAWNMOWER
A BONFIRE STARTING ON THE OTHER SIDE
SIGH

I'M DESPERATELY WORRIED ABOUT THE PRIME MINISTER'S SPEECH TONIGHT...
WILL HE END THE LOCKDOWN?
WHAT WILL HE SAY?
WE'RE NOT READY!
ANOTHER 7 WEEKS?
I WENT FOR A WALK TO TRY TO STOP MYSELF THINKING ABOUT IT...
IT DIDN'T WORK.
MUM ISN'T SAFE
WHAT IF YOU DON'T GET TO SEE ROB UNTIL 2021?
THE PM IS A SELFISH PRICK
I SIT DOWN AND TRY TO JUST LISTEN TO THE SOUNDS OF NATURE
SHHHHHH
WE DON'T HAVE ENOUGH PPE OR TESTS-
SHUT UP
SHHHHH

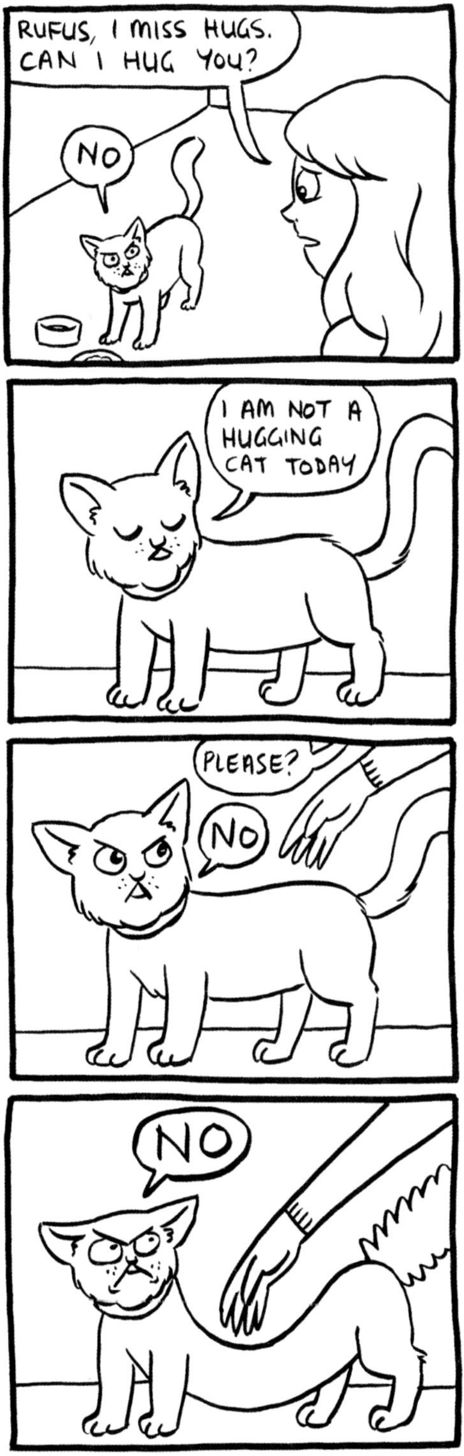
RUFUS, I MISS HUGS. CAN I HUG YOU?
NO
I AM NOT A HUGGING CAT TODAY
PLEASE?
NO
NO

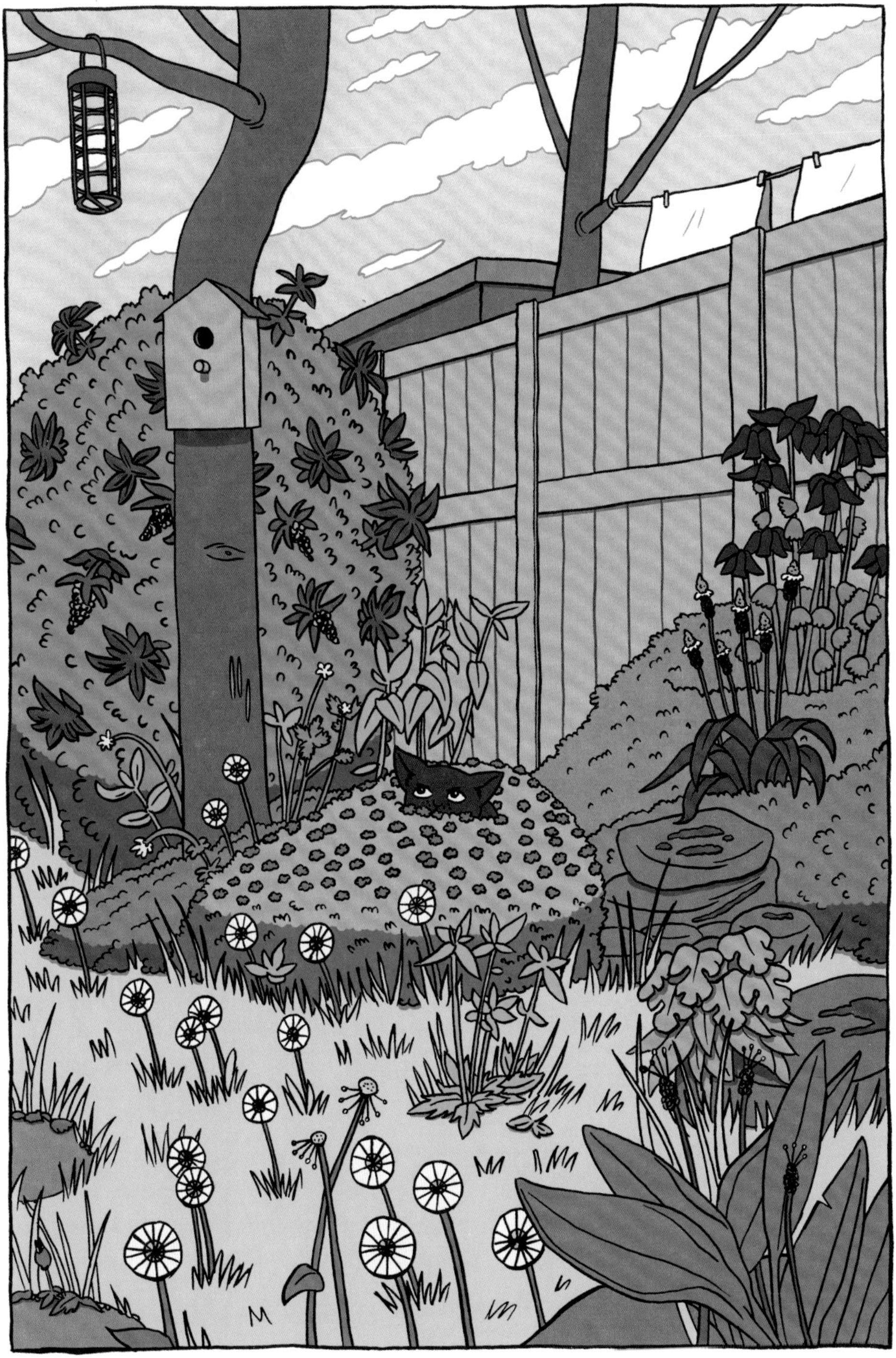

THE PMS SPEECH HAD NOTHING IN IT ABOUT WHEN WE MIGHT BE ABLE TO SEE LOVED ONES.
ALTHOUGH IT DID SAY PEOPLE SHOULD GO BACK TO WORK.
SOME GOING BACK TOMORROW. WITH NO PPE.
SO LONG AS THEY DON'T TRAVEL THERE-
ENOUGH

TODAY IS HARD.

I DON'T REALISE I'M CRYING UNTIL IT DRIPS ONTO THE PAPER I'M DRAWING ON.

IT FEELS LIKE THERE'S NOTHING TO KEEP ME GOING. THERE'S NOTHING GOOD HERE.

I AM STILL HERE

OK...
I'M DECIDING RIGHT NOW...
THAT TODAY WILL BE A GOOD DAY.
STAND
OW.

HA! DON'T WORRY LOVE, I DON'T HAVE IT!
BUT I MIGHT!
REACH
SA
OK, WELL IF YOU DO THEN I'D LIKE TO GET IT! I THINK WE ALL SHOULD!
LIKE HERD IMMUNITY? NO! THAT'S CRAZY!
HA! WELL I WENT TO MEDICAL SCHOOL FOR 29 YEARS SO I DOUBT I AM...
UM... UH... OK...
LATER.
"WELL YOU MUST BE REALLY DUMB 'CAUSE IT'S ONLY MEANT TO TAKE FOUR."
WHY, BRAIN, WHY??
COME UP WITH STUFF FASTER, DAMMIT!!

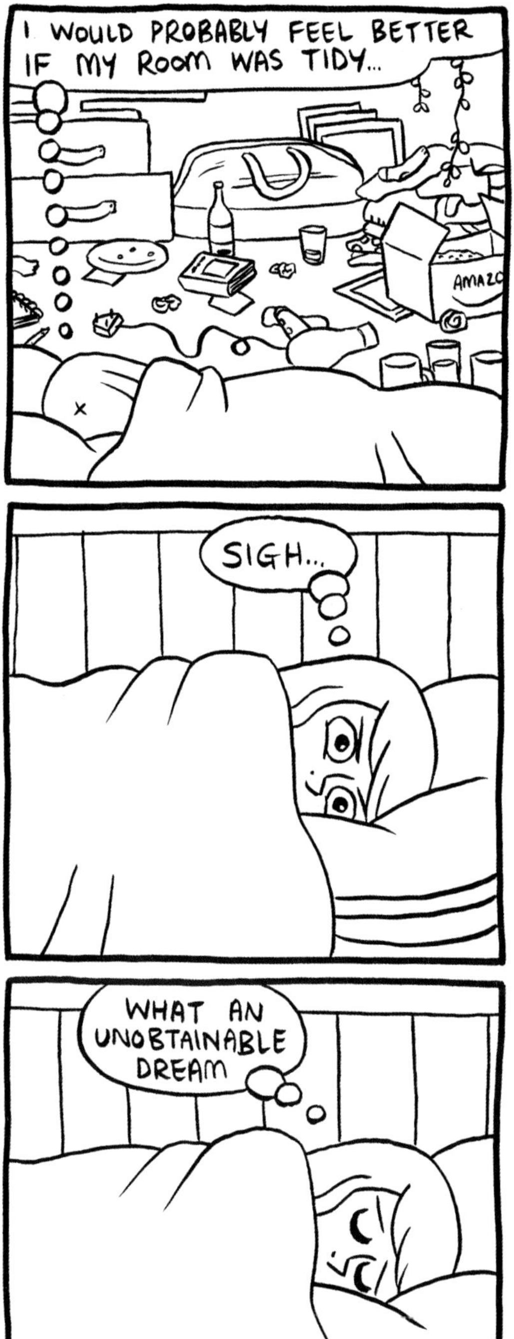
I WOULD PROBABLY FEEL BETTER IF MY ROOM WAS TIDY...
AMAZO
SIGH...
WHAT AN UNOBTAINABLE DREAM

OUR PADDLING POOL CAME!
HAHA! YAYYY!
(DRUNK)
WE SHOULD FILL IT WITH WINE!
I MEAN I'M NOT SAYING "NO"!...
HAHAA

I DREAM THAT ROB AND I HAVE BEEN QUARANTINED TOGETHER IN A HOTEL ROOM...
CENSORED!
IN THE MORNING...
OH...
OH MY... ...
MAYBE I'LL BE ABLE TO HOLD ON TO THESE FEELINGS AND FEEL REALLY SEXY ALL DAY
AAAAND MY PERIOD JUST STARTED

I'M GOING TO HAVE A NAP!!
WHAT A FULL LIFE YOU LEAD
BUT GET THIS - I'M NOT GOING TO SET AN ALARM!
HM
WILL I NAP FOR TWENTY MINUTES? FOUR HOURS? EIGHT HOURS??
NOBODY KNOWS!
NOBODY CARES

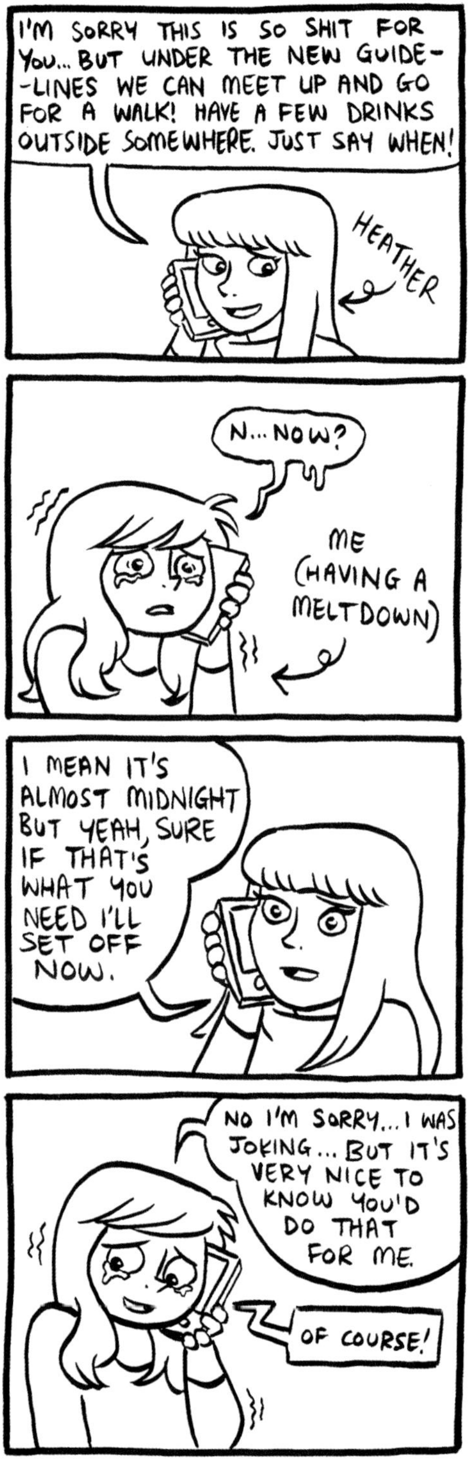

I'M SORRY THIS IS SO SHIT FOR YOU... BUT UNDER THE NEW GUIDE--LINES WE CAN MEET UP AND GO FOR A WALK! HAVE A FEW DRINKS OUTSIDE SOMEWHERE. JUST SAY WHEN!
HEATHER
N... NOW?
ME (HAVING A MELTDOWN)
I MEAN IT'S ALMOST MIDNIGHT BUT YEAH, SURE IF THAT'S WHAT YOU NEED I'LL SET OFF NOW.
NO I'M SORRY... I WAS JOKING... BUT IT'S VERY NICE TO KNOW YOU'D DO THAT FOR ME.
OF COURSE!

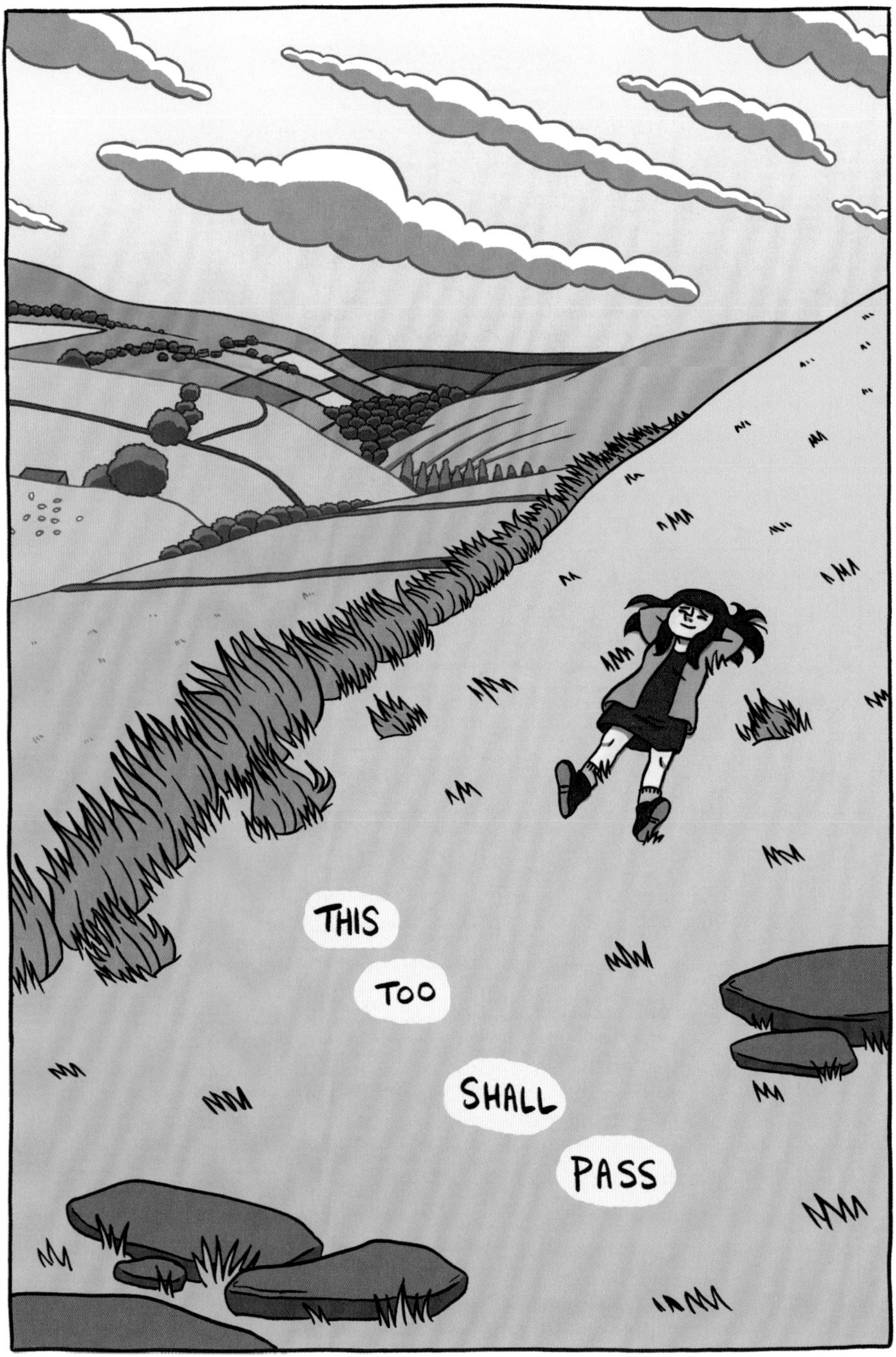
THIS
TOO
SHALL
PASS

HI MUM... YEAH I'M OK! ... MISSING ROB A LOT... AND YOU OF COURSE!...
DARLING I WANTED TO ASK ABOUT YOUR ANTI-DEPRESSANTS...
WELL, I'M STILL ON THEM BUT ONLY EVERY OTHER DAY. HONESTLY MUM DON'T WORRY ABOUT ME.
I'LL CALL THE DOCS IF I STRUGGLE. I'M KEEPING BUSY WITH WORK AND STUFF.
I KNOW YOU ARE, LOVE. I THINK YOU'RE DOING SO WELL. I'M REALLY PROUD OF YOU.
AW... THANKS MUM!
EVEN AT THE RIPE OLD AGE OF 35...
YOUR MUM TELLING YOU SHE'S PROUD OF YOU IS STILL THE BEST

LOCKDOWN TIP: IF YOU SLEEP IN PAST 12 PM...
YOU ONLY HAVE TO FEED YOURSELF TWICE PER DAY!
MIGHT I SUGGEST TOAST FOR EVERY MEAL!
PLEASE LET ME COOK FOR YOU...

ROB: GOT MY CAR WORKING AGAIN!
ME: COOL!
ROB: SO... SEE YOU IN AN HOUR?
ROB IS COMING TO SEE ME!!
ROB IS COMING TO SEE ME!!
ROB IS COMING TO SEE ME!

ROB, IAIN, RACHEL, AND I ALL HAD A SOCIALLY-DISTANCED SIT IN THE GARDEN
IAIN
ROB
RACHEL
ME
IT WAS REALLY HARD NOT TO BE ABLE TO HUG/KISS HIM... BUT IT WAS LOVELY TO BE IN THE SAME SPACE AS HIM.
I WAS GLAD RACHEL AND IAIN WERE THERE... I THINK THAT STOPPED ME FROM DOING ANYTHING STUPID...
OH NO! LOOK AT ME *ACCIDENTALLY* FALLING INTO YOUR ARMS!!
EEP!
JUMP

AMERICA KEEPS TALKING ABOUT "OPENING UP."

WHICH SOUNDS REALLY LOVELY IN A WAY! LIKE A FLOWER BLOOMING!

BUT ACTUALLY IT'S VERY SCARY.

IT'S TOO SOON...

I DON'T WANT THIS... FOR ANY OF US...

SINCE THE VIRUS STARTED, I'VE FOUND IT SUPER DIFFICULT TO FOCUS ON ANYTHING...

EVEN THINGS I ENJOY...

VIDEO GAMES, ONE OF MY FAVOURITE HOBBIES, HAVE BECOME IMPOSSIBLE.

SAME FOR COOKING, OR WATCHING NEW SHOWS ON TV / NETFLIX...

I CAN SOMETIMES READ IN THE EVENINGS, BUT IT'S VERY, VERY SLOW-GOING...

IT'S AS IF THE FEAR OF COVID-19 HAS TAKEN UP SO MUCH OF MY BRAIN...I CAN'T FIT MUCH OF ANYTHING ELSE IN...

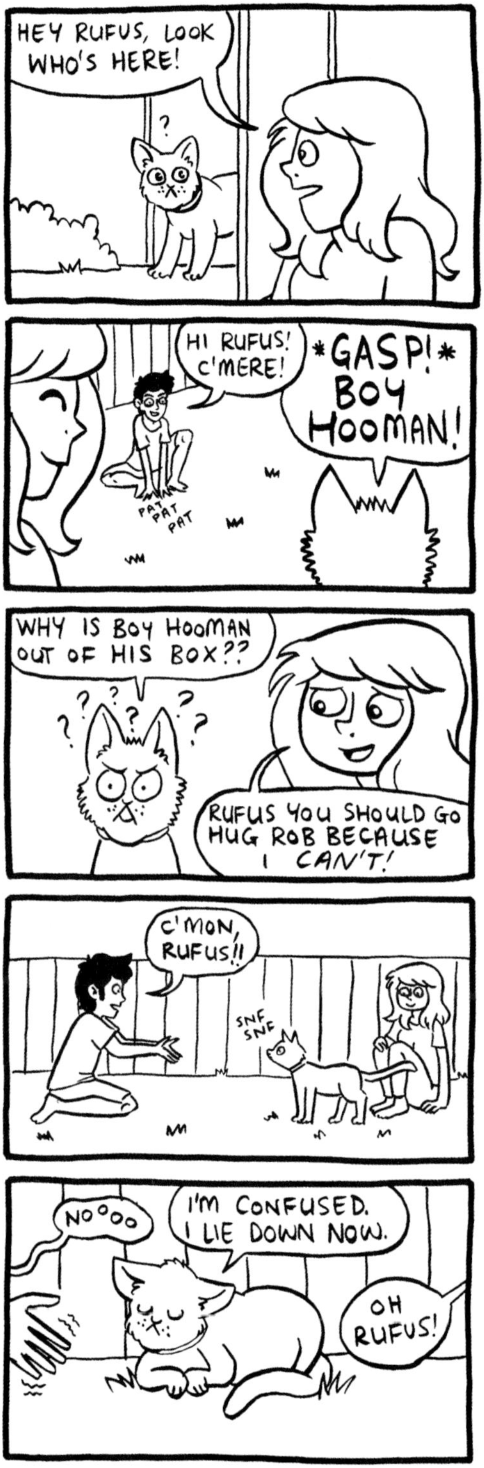
HEY RUFUS, LOOK WHO'S HERE!
?
HI RUFUS! C'MERE!
GASP! BOY HOOMAN!
PAT PAT PAT
WHY IS BOY HOOMAN OUT OF HIS BOX??
RUFUS YOU SHOULD GO HUG ROB BECAUSE I CAN'T!
C'MON, RUFUS!!
SNF SNF
NOooo
I'M CONFUSED. I LIE DOWN NOW.
OH RUFUS!

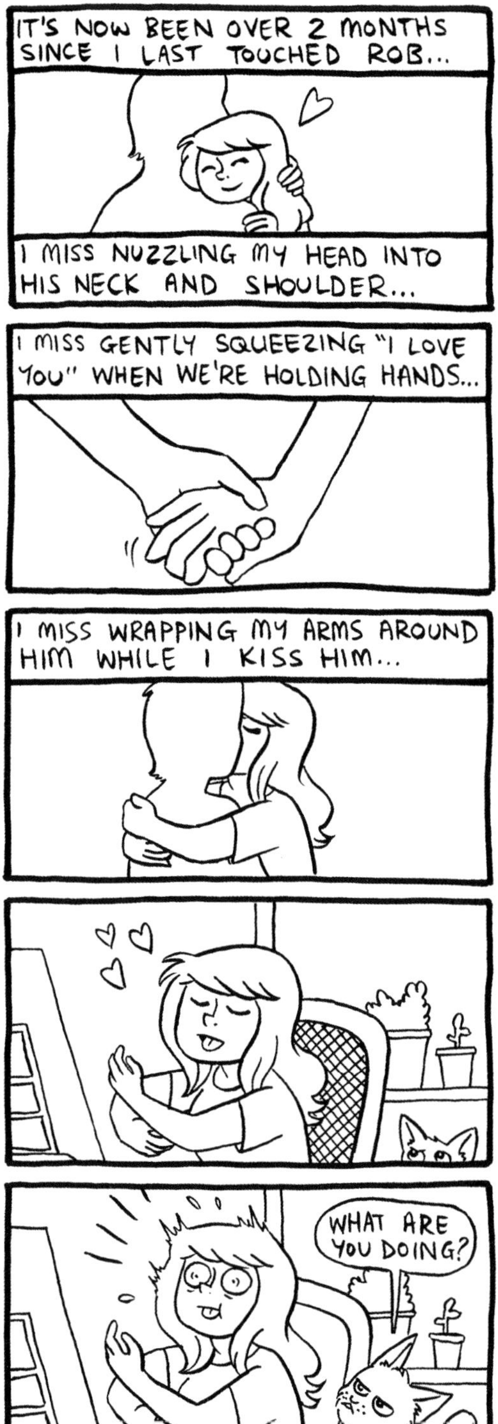
IT'S NOW BEEN OVER 2 MONTHS SINCE I LAST TOUCHED ROB...
I MISS NUZZLING MY HEAD INTO HIS NECK AND SHOULDER...
I MISS GENTLY SQUEEZING "I LOVE YOU" WHEN WE'RE HOLDING HANDS...
I MISS WRAPPING MY ARMS AROUND HIM WHILE I KISS HIM...
WHAT ARE YOU DOING?

I'VE BEEN STRUGGLING THIS PAST WEEK AND I THINK RUFUS HAS NOTICED...

HE'S BEEN FOLLOWING ME AROUND A LOT MORE...

AT BEDTIME HE'S BEEN SLEEPING ON MY CHEST INSTEAD OF DOWN BY MY FEET...

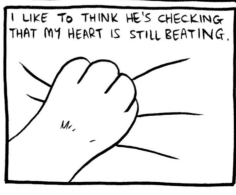

I LIKE TO THINK HE'S CHECKING THAT MY HEART IS STILL BEATING.

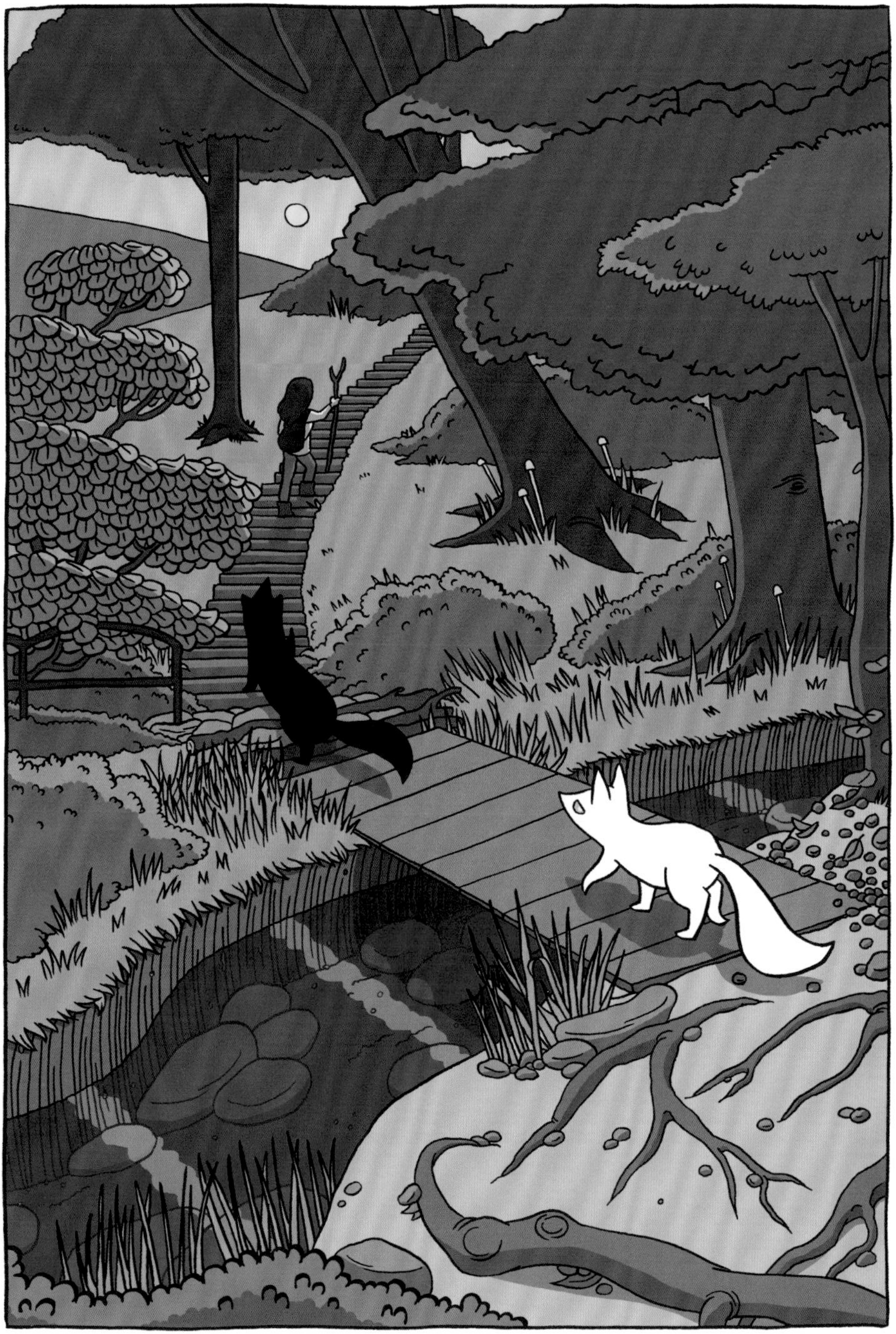

I DREAMED THAT I PEELED AWAY ALL MY SKIN...
AND UNDERNEATH WAS A COMPLETELY DIFFERENT PERSON...
?
?
?
?
I LOVED IT.
I WISH I COULD TAKE A BREAK FROM BEING ME.

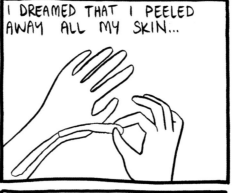

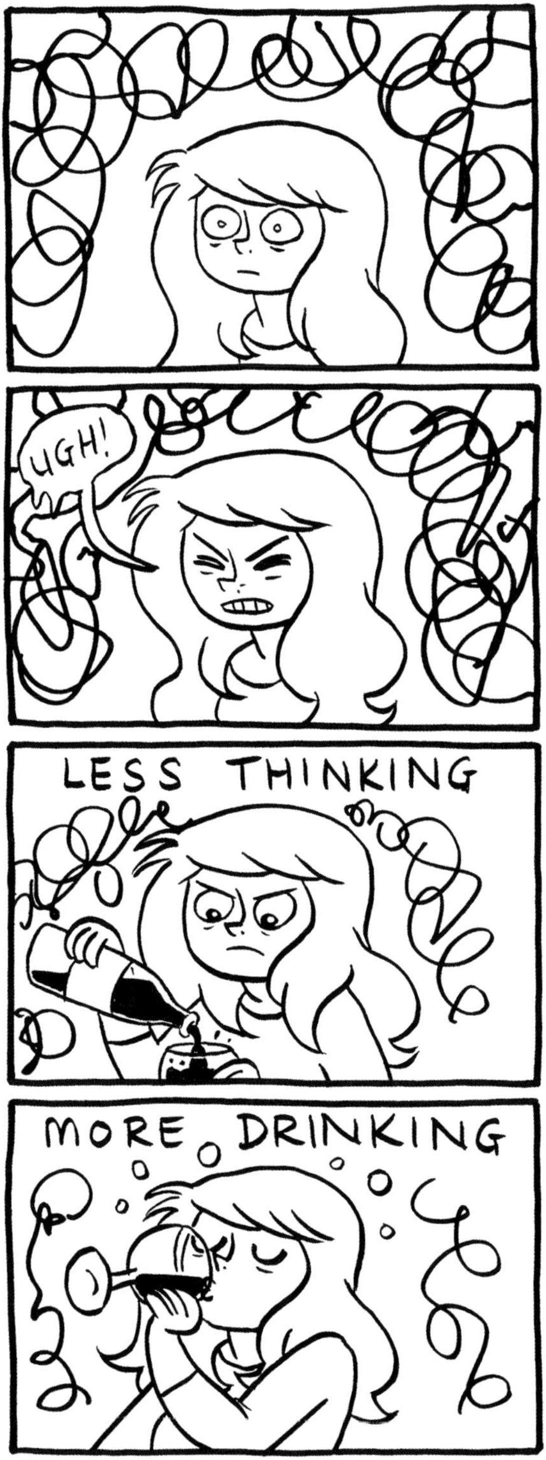

UGH!
LESS THINKING
MORE DRINKING

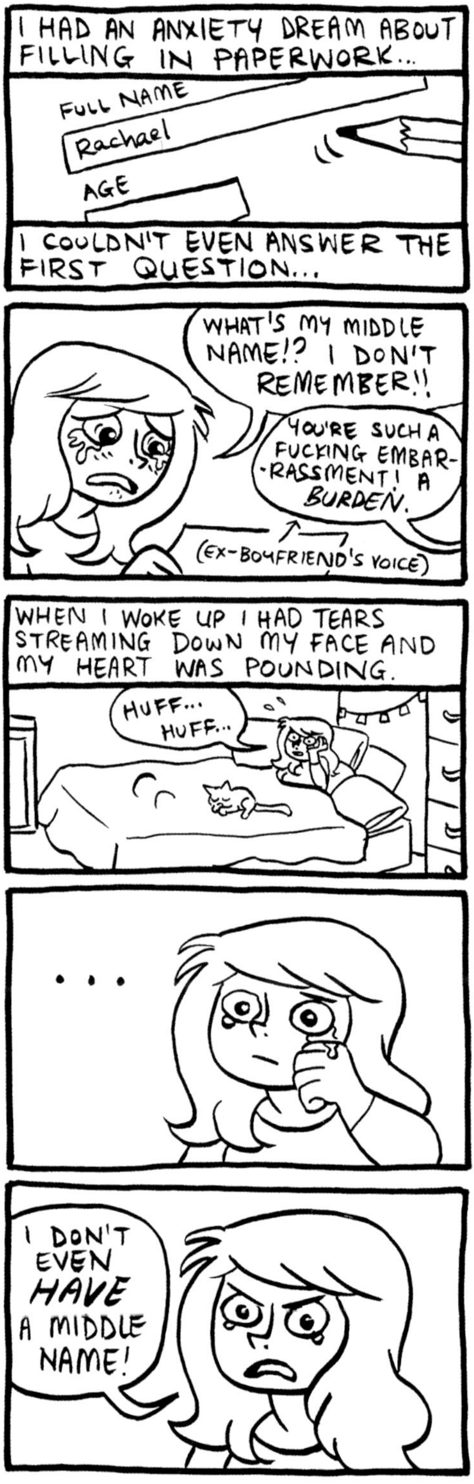
I HAD AN ANXIETY DREAM ABOUT FILLING IN PAPERWORK...
FULL NAME
Rachael
AGE
I COULDN'T EVEN ANSWER THE FIRST QUESTION...
WHAT'S MY MIDDLE NAME!? I DON'T REMEMBER!!
YOU'RE SUCH A FUCKING EMBAR-RASSMENT! A BURDEN.
(EX-BOYFRIEND'S VOICE)
WHEN I WOKE UP I HAD TEARS STREAMING DOWN MY FACE AND MY HEART WAS POUNDING.
HUFF... HUFF...
...
I DON'T EVEN HAVE A MIDDLE NAME!

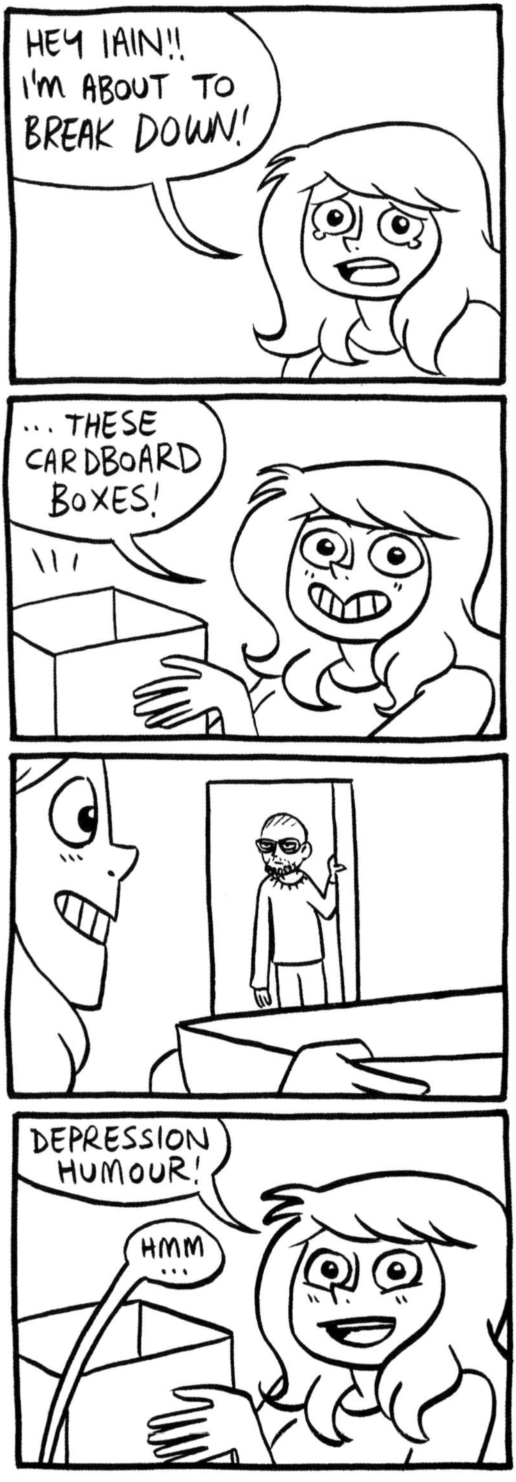
HEY IAIN!! I'M ABOUT TO BREAK DOWN!
... THESE CARDBOARD BOXES!
DEPRESSION HUMOUR!
HMM...

IN THE GARDEN I FOUND A LITTLE BEE WITH BROKEN WINGS...
IT KEPT TRYING TO FLY, BUT IT COULDN'T DO IT...
I GAVE IT A TEASPOON OF HONEY, WHICH IT LAPPED UP...
Nom
NOT KNOWING WHAT ELSE TO DO, I LEFT IT TO ITS MEAL, BUT THAT NIGHT I WORRIED...
WHAT IF IT RAINS?
SHOULD I HAVE BROUGHT IT INSIDE?
I DON'T KNOW THE FIRST THING ABOUT CARING FOR A BEE...
HOW WILL IT FIND ITS HIVE AGAIN?
IS IT SILLY TO LOSE SLEEP OVER A LITTLE BEE?
UGHHHH...

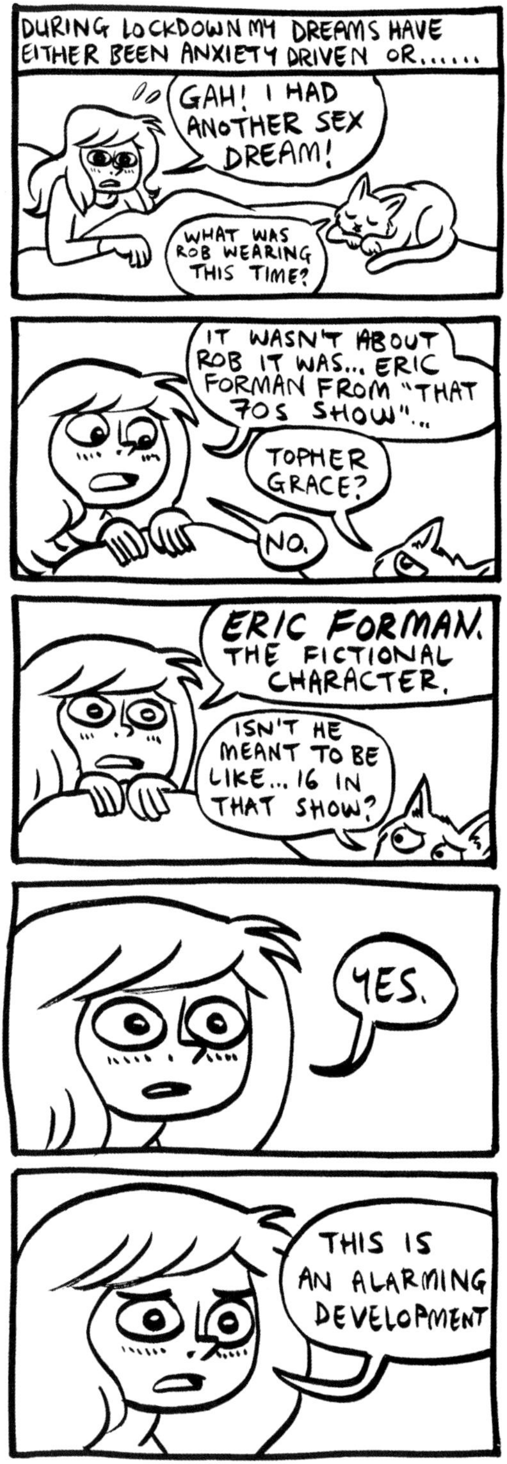
DURING LOCKDOWN MY DREAMS HAVE EITHER BEEN ANXIETY DRIVEN OR......
GAH! I HAD ANOTHER SEX DREAM!
WHAT WAS ROB WEARING THIS TIME?
IT WASN'T ABOUT ROB IT WAS... ERIC FORMAN FROM "THAT 70S SHOW"...
TOPHER GRACE?
NO.
ERIC FORMAN. THE FICTIONAL CHARACTER.
ISN'T HE MEANT TO BE LIKE... 16 IN THAT SHOW?
YES.
THIS IS AN ALARMING DEVELOPMENT

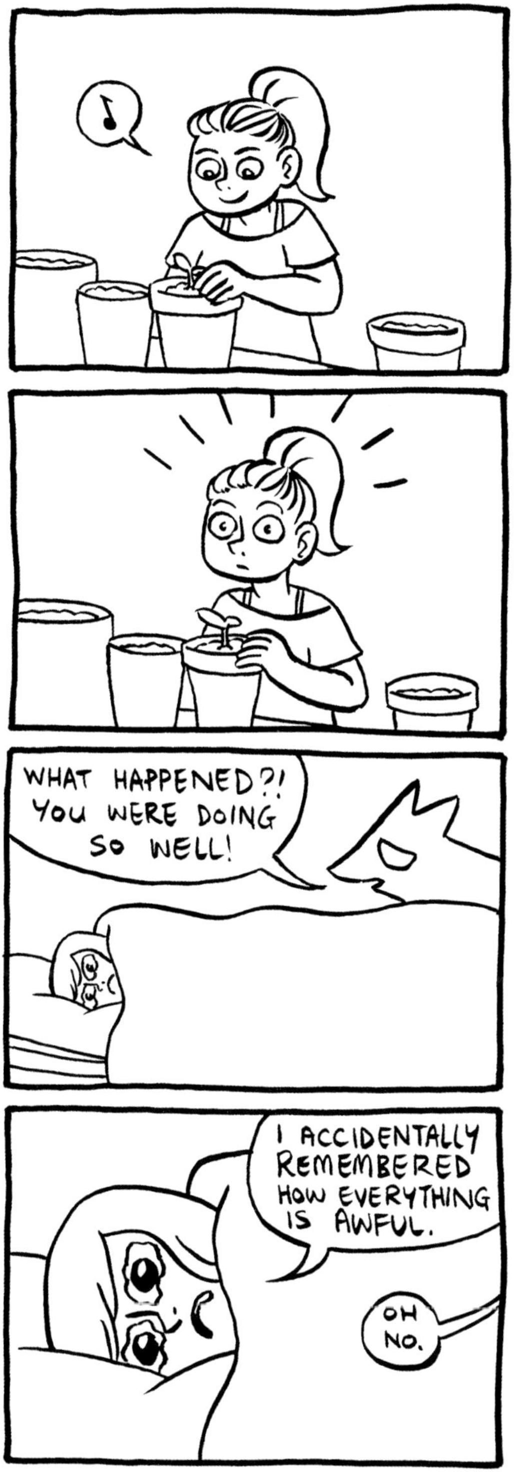
WHAT HAPPENED?! YOU WERE DOING SO WELL!
I ACCIDENTALLY REMEMBERED HOW EVERYTHING IS AWFUL.
OH NO.

WHY AM I MAKING THESE STUPID COMICS?
THEY GIVE YOU A REASON TO GET UP IN THE MORNING.
IT'S NOT LIKE I'M GONNA SAVE ANYONE WITH THEM. I'M BEING SELFISH JUST DOING THEM SO THAT I HAVE PURPOSE.
RACHAEL. EVEN IF YOUR COMICS SAVE JUST ONE PERSON... THAT'S OK
IT'S ALSO OK IF THAT ONE PERSON IS YOU.

I'VE PUT ON A BIT OF WEIGHT SINCE LOCKDOWN... BUT I'M KINDA FEELIN' IT! MY BOOBS AND BUTT ARE LOOKING GREAT! YEEAH! LOVE YOURSELF, GIRL!
Literally 2 minutes later...
I AM A LITERAL WHALE! I HATE MY STUPID SELF!!

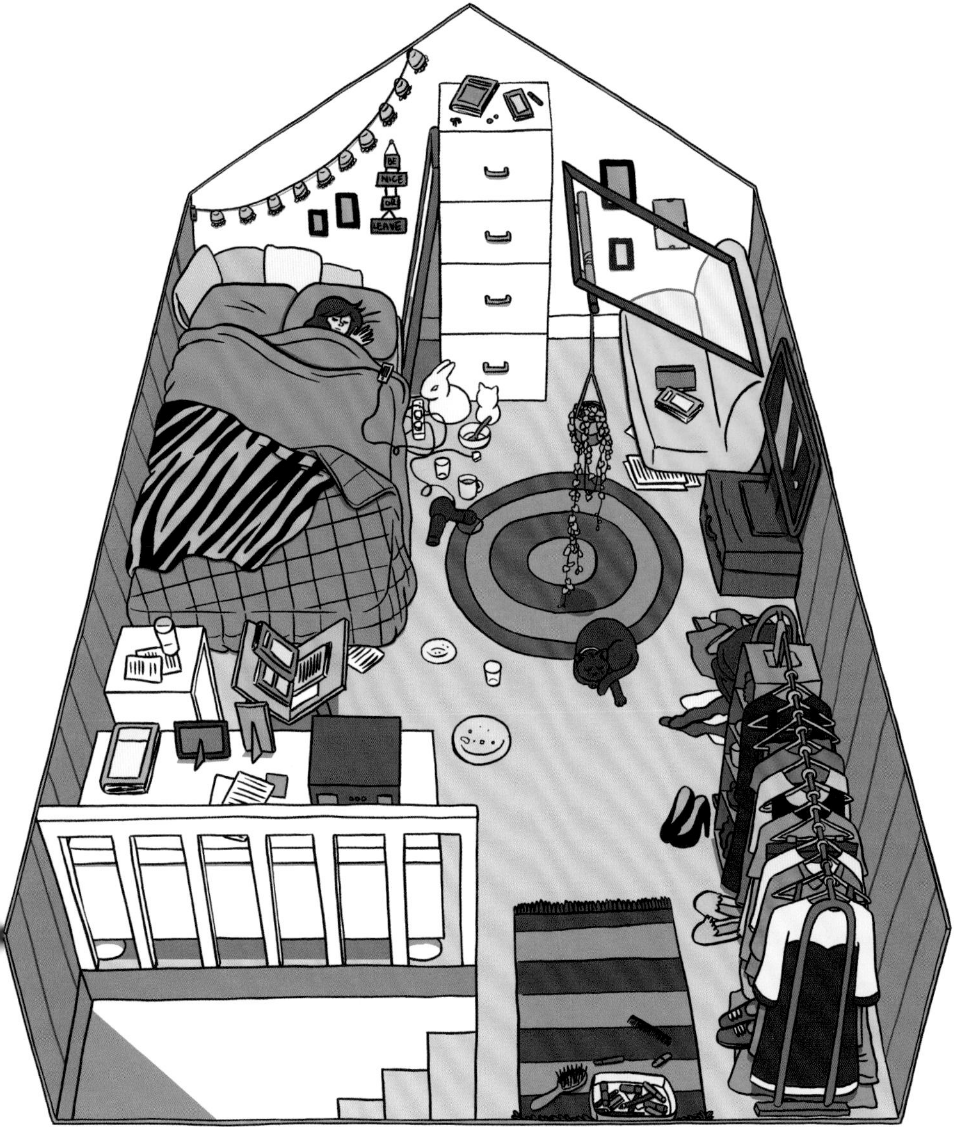
BE
NICE
OR
LEAVE

I'VE FALLEN IN LOVE WITH GROWING SUCCULENTS. FROM PUTTING THE LEAVES ON A DAMP PIECE OF KITCHEN ROLL...
...TO POTTING THEM IN COMPOST WHEN THEY SPROUT THEIR ROOTS...
THE ONLY PROBLEM IS... LIKE WITH MANY THINGS IN MY LIFE...
I JUST DON'T KNOW WHEN TO STOP.
HMM...

H-HELLO...
NERVOUS PAT
SNORT!!
TEE HEE!
PAT PAT PAT

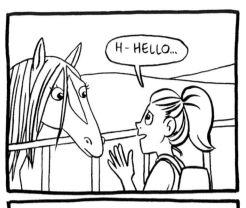

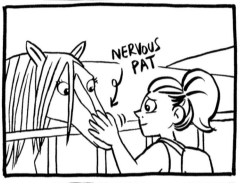

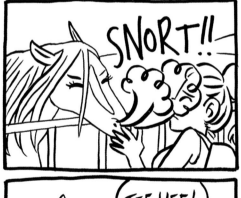

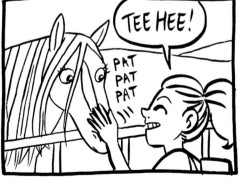

SO HOW WAS THAT WALK FOR YOU- EASY? HARD?
IT WAS PRETTY EASY! I FEEL GOOD!
HEATHER
THAT'S GREAT!
NOW THAT I KNOW HOW MUCH STAMINA YOU HAVE I'M GONNA REALLY FUCK YOU UP TOMORROW.
HAHAHA!
YAAAAAAYY...

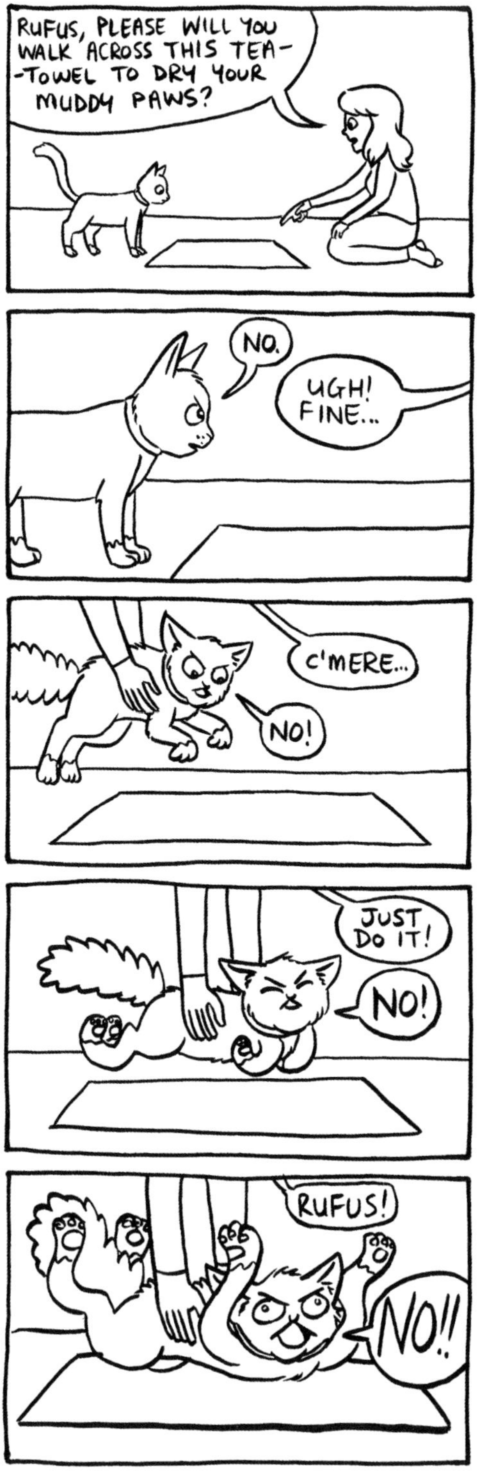
RUFUS, PLEASE WILL YOU WALK ACROSS THIS TEA--TOWEL TO DRY YOUR MUDDY PAWS?
NO.
UGH! FINE...
C'MERE...
NO!
JUST DO IT!
NO!
RUFUS!
NO!!

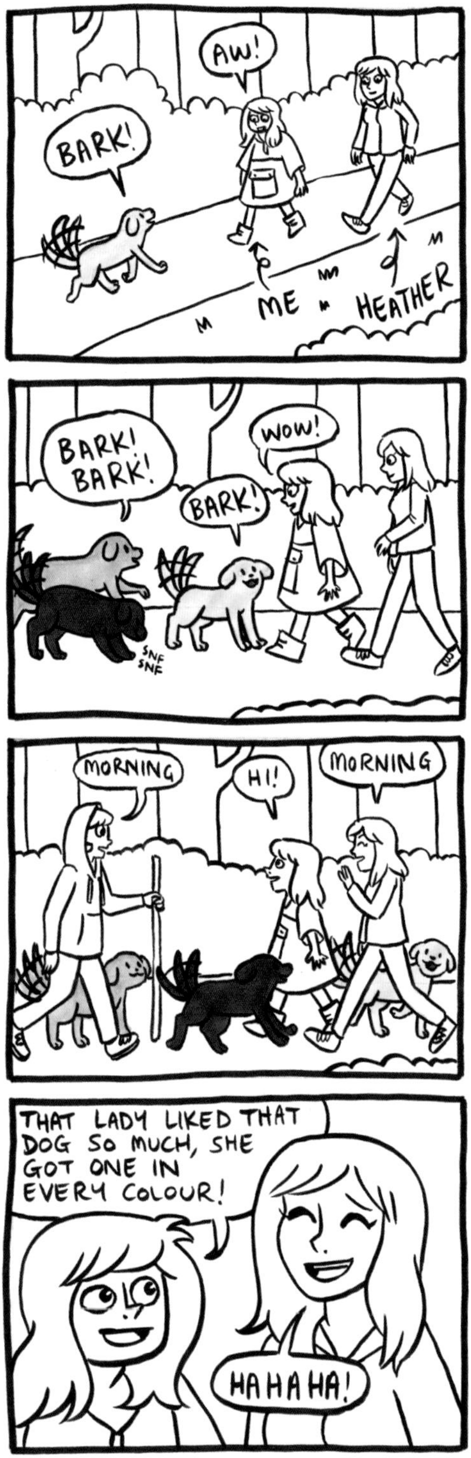
BARK!
AW!
ME
HEATHER
BARK! BARK!
BARK!
WOW!
SNF SNF
MORNING
HI!
MORNING
THAT LADY LIKED THAT DOG SO MUCH, SHE GOT ONE IN EVERY COLOUR!
HAHAHA!

ON JUNE 2nd IT WAS #blackouttuesday AND LOTS OF SOCIAL MEDIA ACCOUNTS POSTED BLACK SQUARES INSTEAD OF THEIR USUAL CONTENT.
IT'S A NICE GESTURE, BUT SOMETHING ABOUT IT SEEMED A BIT SHALLOW... ALL THESE ACCOUNTS ARE JUST GOING TO GO BACK TO NORMAL THE NEXT DAY.
WE CAN DO BETTER. DONATE TO BLACK CHARITIES, EDUCATE YOURSELF, PROTEST, LISTEN. CALL OUT RACIST BEHAVIOUR WHEREVER YOU SEE IT, EVEN IF IT COMES FROM FRIENDS OR LOVED ONES.
DONATION RECIE
$20
THANK YOU!
ESPECIALLY THEN.
WE NEED TO DO BETTER.

I MISS YOUR TOUCH SO BADLY.
NOT JUST IN A SEXUAL WAY.
IN A "RANDOM KISS ON THE SHOULDER" WAY.
SMEK
IN A "YOUR HAIR LOOKS NICE" WAY.
IN A "I'M RIGHT HERE" WAY.

WHY DO I FEEL SO SHITTY?
BECAUSE YOU SPENT THE WHOLE DAY INDOORS LOOKING AT SCREENS, EATING CRAP AND NOT DRINKING WATER.
IT'S SUCH A MYSTERY...
SIGH

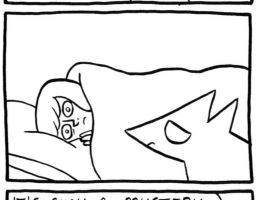

HEY BABE, HOW'S YOUR DAY GOING?
I CRIED IN THE WOODS AND THEN HAD A 3 HOUR SADNESS NAP.
WOULD IT HELP IF I DROVE OVER AND SAT IN YOUR GARDEN WITH YOU?
YES. YES IT WOULD.

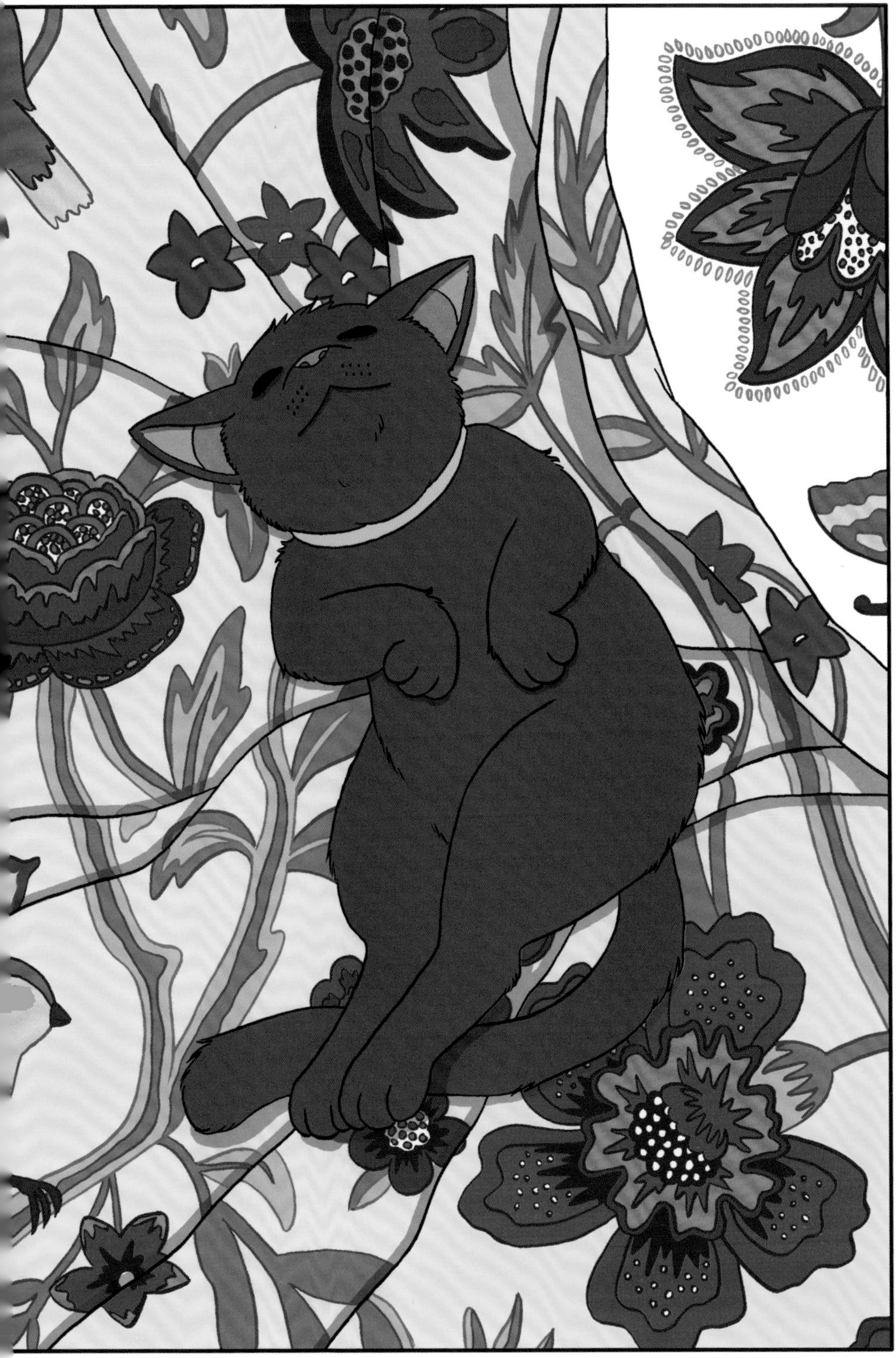

HEATHER'S BEEN CONCERNED ABOUT MY MENTAL HEALTH, SO SHE'S BEEN TAKING ME OUT FOR WALKS MOST MORNINGS...
I'LL BE ROUND IN 20 MINS!
YOU'RE NOT ACTUALLY GOING ARE YOU?
SHE CALLS THESE WALKS "THE RACHAEL SERATONIN CHECKS"...
SO HOW WE DOING TODAY?
I LIKE HOW SIMPLE IT ALL FEELS WHEN WE'RE WALKING...
OR, AS HEATHER PUTS IT:
JUST PUT ONE FOOT IN FRONT OF THE OTHER UNTIL THINGS FEEL LESS SHIT.

BORIS JOHNSON FINALLY ANNOUNCED THE IDEA OF "BUBBLES" AND I GOT EXCITED THAT I'D FINALLY BE ABLE TO HUG ROB ...TO *KISS* ROB... TO.. *AHEM*...

BUT ROB AND I BOTH HAVE HOUSEMATES, AND UNDER THE NEW RULES ONE OF US WOULD HAVE TO LIVE ALONE FOR US TO BE ABLE TO TOUCH EACH OTHER...

I ASKED ROB IF WE COULD IGNORE THAT BIT BUT HE SAID NO. I WAS SAD BUT ALSO PROUD THAT HE HAS SO MUCH INTEGRITY AND A REAL WANT TO DO THE RIGHT THING...

IF HE DIDN'T HAVE THOSE QUALITIES HE WOULDN'T BE ROB, AND I WOULDN'T BE SO HOPELESSLY IN LOVE WITH HIM...

BUT STILL... GOD DAMN IT!!

NEW YEARS EVE, 2019
HEY.
WHO ARE YOU?
I'M YOU, BUT 5 MONTHS FROM NOW. HOW YOU DOING?
OH, Y'KNOW... HAVING MY NYE PANIC ABOUT WHETHER I'M A GOOD PERSON...
FORGET THAT. I NEED YOU TO REALLY ENJOY THE NEXT 2 MONTHS, OK?
WHY? WHAT HAPPENS?
I CAN'T TELL YOU MUCH BUT... THINGS GET WEIRD. TRUST ME...
PFFT... HOW WEIRD COULD IT GET IN JUST 5 MONTHS?
I'M CURRENTLY WAITING FOR BORIS JOHNSON TO TELL ME WHEN I'M ALLOWED TO HAVE SEX WITH MY BOYFRIEND.
ARE YOU DRUNK!?
OF COURSE I'M DRUNK! IT'S 2020!!

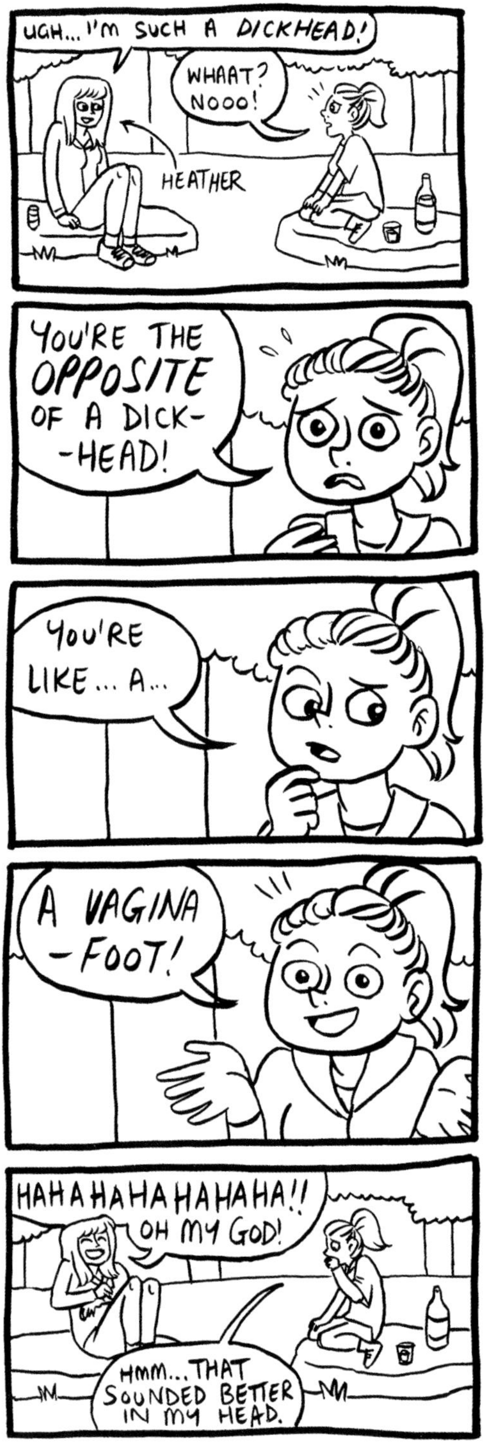
UGH... I'M SUCH A DICKHEAD!
WHAAT? NOOO!
HEATHER
YOU'RE THE OPPOSITE OF A DICK-HEAD!
YOU'RE LIKE... A...
A VAGINA-FOOT!
HAHAHAHAHAHAHAHA!! OH MY GOD!
HMM... THAT SOUNDED BETTER IN MY HEAD.

ROB TELLS ME EXCITING NEWS: HIS HOUSE-MATE IS MOVING OUT IN 3 WEEKS TIME. WHEN THAT HAPPENS WE'LL BE ABLE TO BE IN THE SAME "BUBBLE"...
TIME HAS BEEN A WEIRD CONCEPT SINCE LOCKDOWN BEGAN...
I'VE BEEN AWAKE FOR 10 MINUTES!
IT IS TOMORROW NOW
THE NEXT 3 WEEKS COULD EITHER FEEL LIKE 20 MINUTES OR 7 YEARS.
REMEMBER WHEN APRIL HAD, LIKE, 200 DAYS IN IT?
JUNE

RACHEL CAME OVER TO THE GARDEN
GASP IT PRETTY GIRL HOOMAN!
ARE YOU GOING TO SHOW OFF IN FRONT OF RACHEL AGAIN, RUFUS?
DON'T KNOW WAT MEAN...
SO ANYWAY... I WAS SAYING TO JACK-
I PROTEC YOU FROM DIS!
OH RUFUS...
RAARGH
OY!
WOW

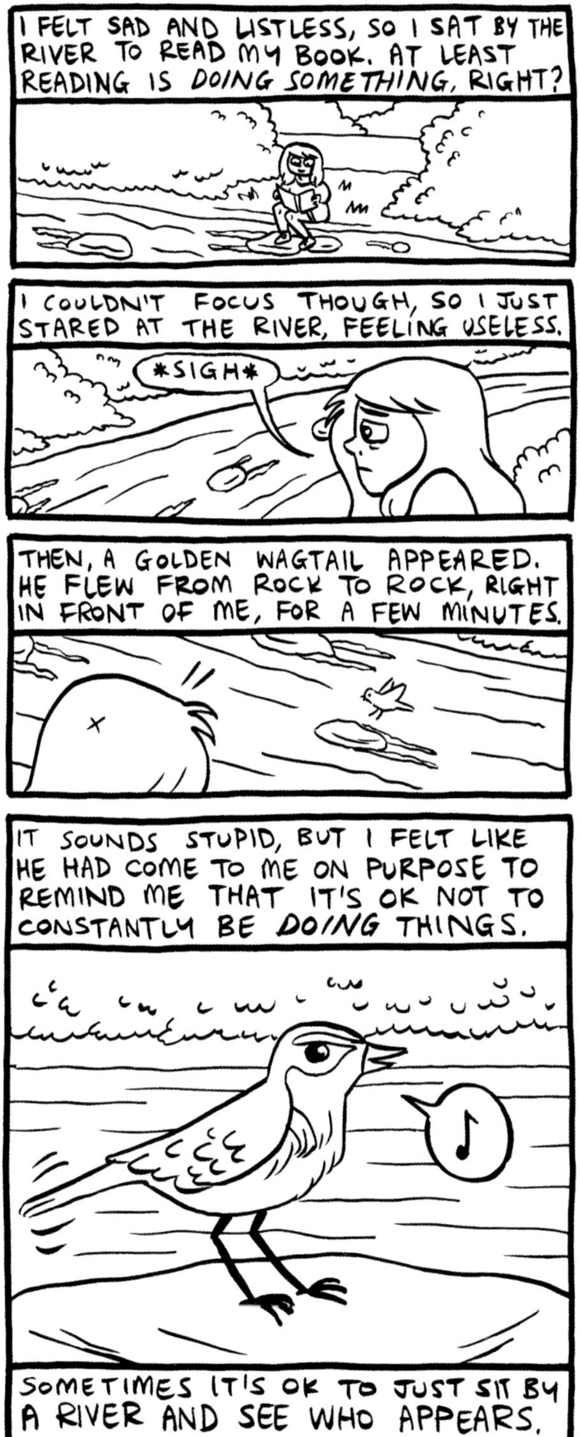

I FELT SAD AND LISTLESS, SO I SAT BY THE RIVER TO READ MY BOOK. AT LEAST READING IS *DOING SOMETHING*, RIGHT?
I COULDN'T FOCUS THOUGH, SO I JUST STARED AT THE RIVER, FEELING USELESS.
SIGH
THEN, A GOLDEN WAGTAIL APPEARED. HE FLEW FROM ROCK TO ROCK, RIGHT IN FRONT OF ME, FOR A FEW MINUTES.
IT SOUNDS STUPID, BUT I FELT LIKE HE HAD COME TO ME ON PURPOSE TO REMIND ME THAT IT'S OK NOT TO CONSTANTLY BE *DOING* THINGS.
♪
SOMETIMES IT'S OK TO JUST SIT BY A RIVER AND SEE WHO APPEARS.

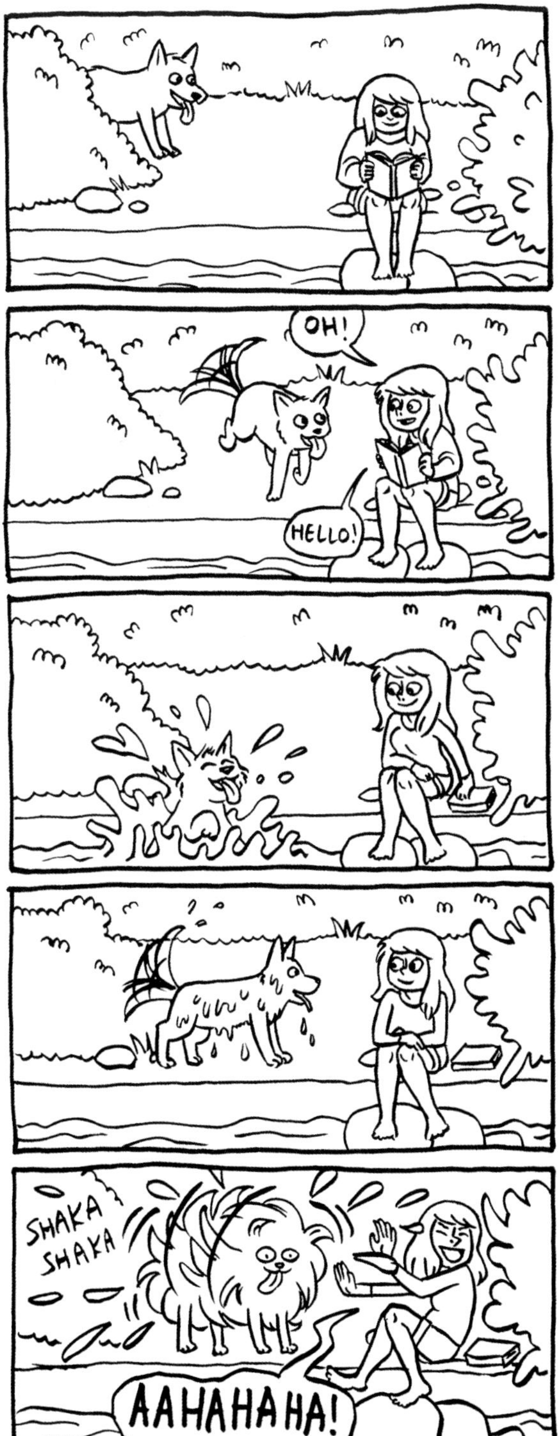
OH!
HELLO!
SHAKA
SHAKA
AAHAHAHA!

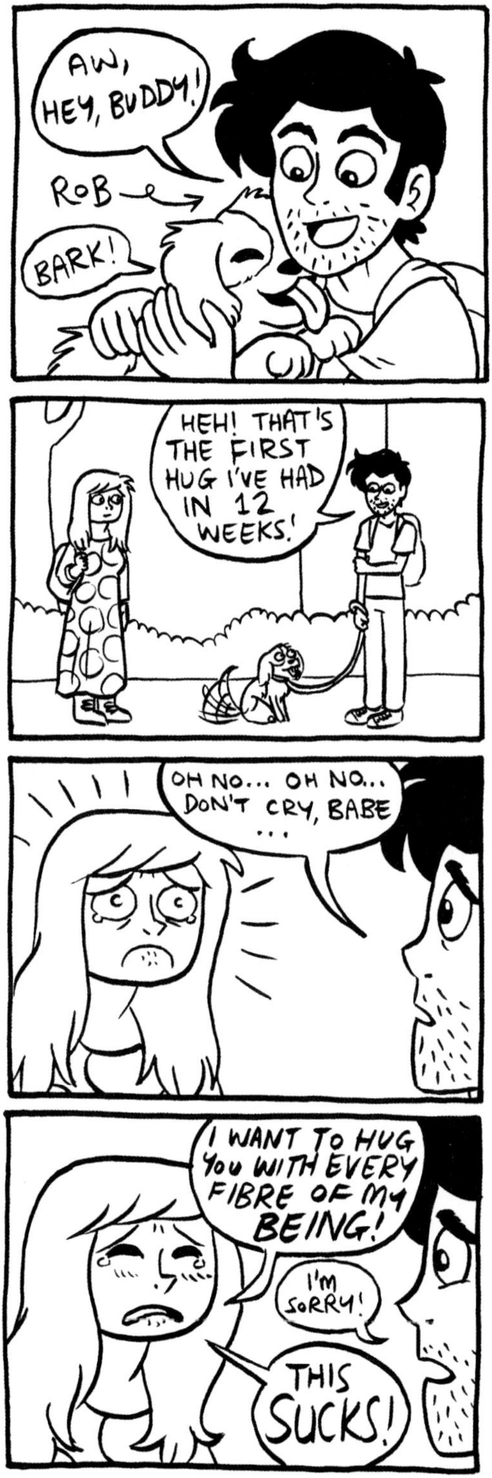
AW, HEY, BUDDY!
ROB
BARK!
HEH! THAT'S THE FIRST HUG I'VE HAD IN 12 WEEKS!
OH NO... OH NO... DON'T CRY, BABE ...
I WANT TO HUG YOU WITH EVERY FIBRE OF MY BEING!
I'M SORRY!
THIS SUCKS!

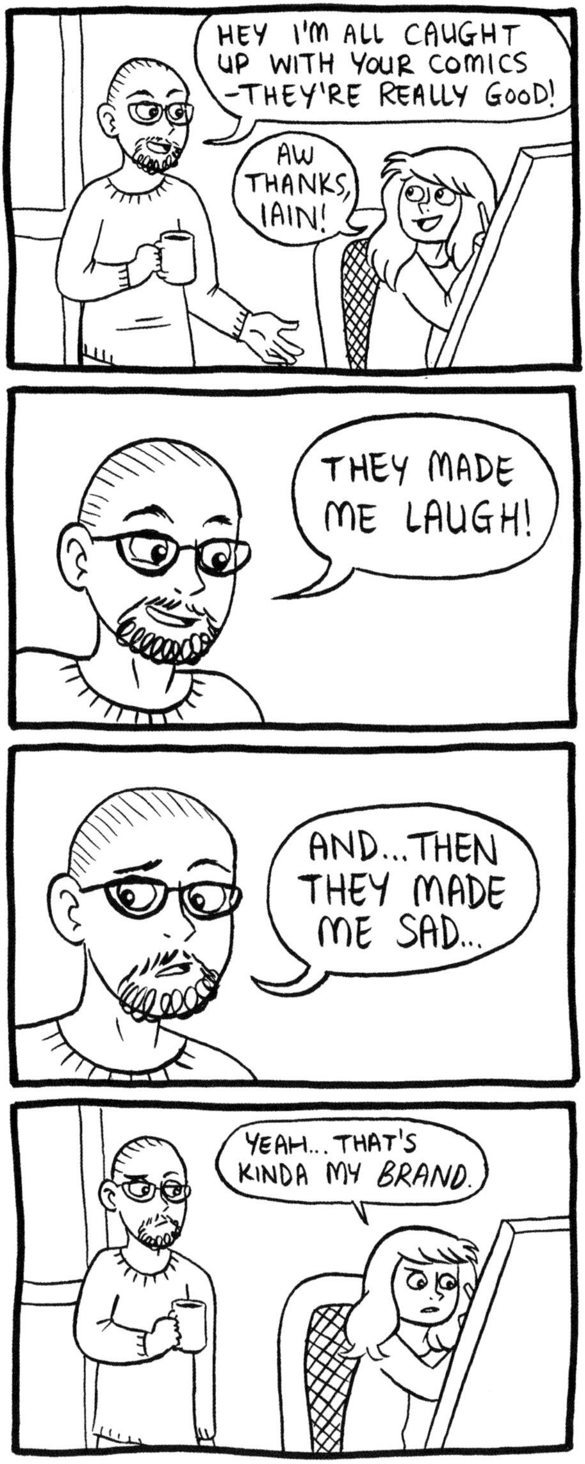
HEY I'M ALL CAUGHT UP WITH YOUR COMICS -THEY'RE REALLY GOOD!
AW THANKS, IAIN!
THEY MADE ME LAUGH!
AND... THEN THEY MADE ME SAD...
YEAH... THAT'S KINDA MY *BRAND*.

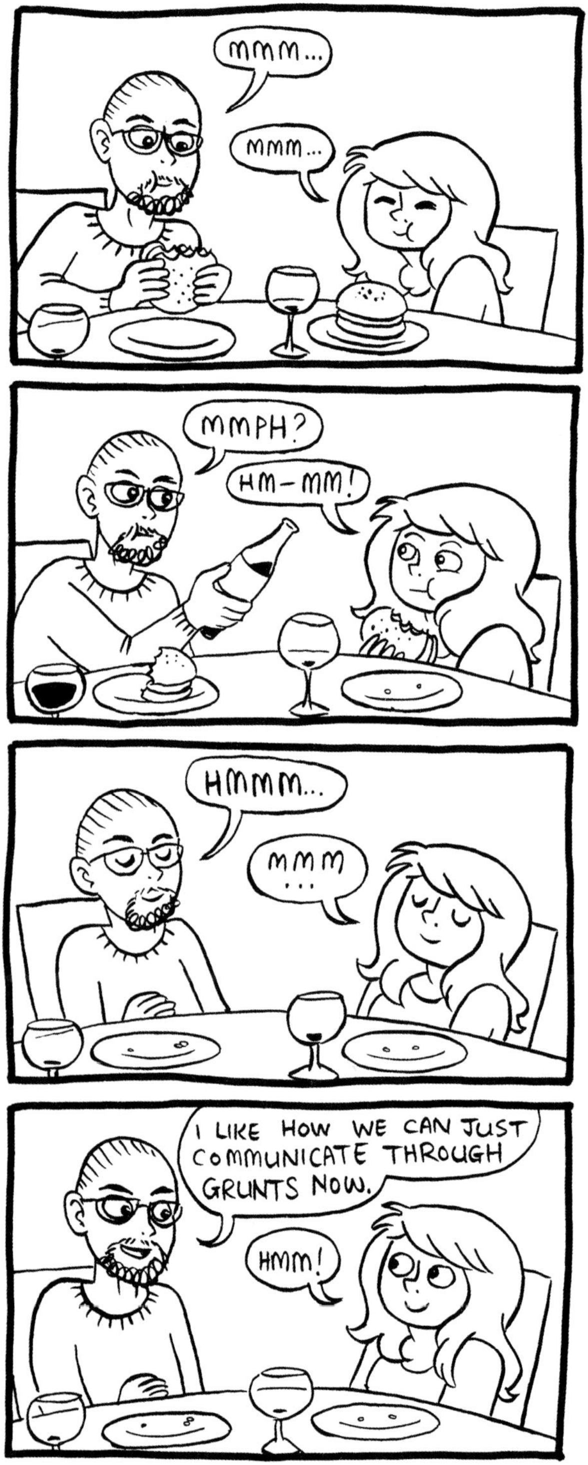
mmm...
mmm...
MMPH?
HM-MM!
HMMM...
MMM ...
I LIKE HOW WE CAN JUST COMMUNICATE THROUGH GRUNTS NOW.
HMM!

STEBBEN (HEATHER'S PARTNER) TOOK ME ON MY FIRST *PROPER* WILD SWIM AND I LOVED EVERYTHING ABOUT IT.
THE COLDNESS OF THE WATER KNOCKING THE AIR OUT OF ME.
OF KNOWING I CAN'T STOP: I HAVE TO KEEP GOING.
THE FEELING OF NOT KNOWING HOW DEEP IT IS... OR WHAT LURKS BENEATH ME.
THE DULL ACHE OF MY SHOCKED MUSCLES AS I PULL MYSELF OUT.
THAT IS *LITERALLY* EVERYTHING I HATE ABOUT IT!
HEATHER (WHO DID NOT WILD SWIM!)

DURING MY WILD SWIM I SAW A BEE DROWNING. I DIDN'T PICK IT OUT AS I DIDN'T THINK I'D BE ABLE TO MAKE IT TO THE STEPS WITH JUST ONE ARM.

I FELT REALLY GUILTY.

AFTERWARDS...

I COULD HAVE PUT IT ON MY HEAD! WHY DIDN'T I DO THAT??

HEATHER

I DUNNO RACH... YOU MIGHT HAVE SCARED IT TO *DEATH*

IMAGINE JUST HAVING A NICE SWIM AND THEN A BIG PEACH GIANT SUDDENLY WEARS YOU AS A *HAT*

I'VE NEVER BEEN DESCRIBED AS A *PEACH GIANT* BEFORE... I LIKE IT!

HAHA! YOU'RE WELCOME!

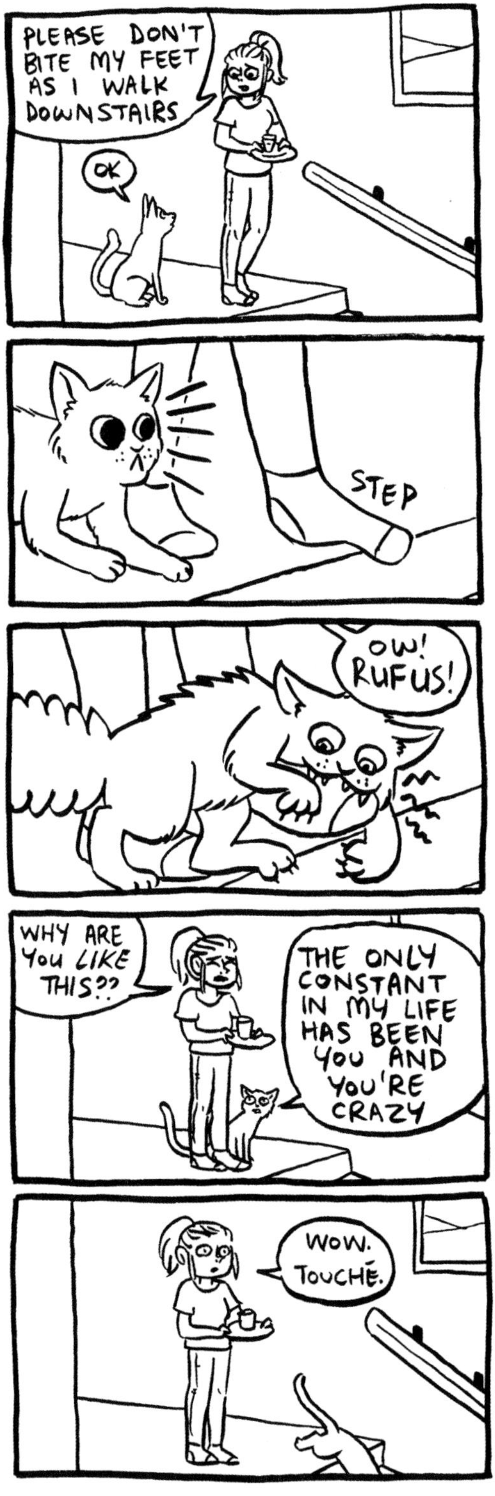
PLEASE DON'T BITE MY FEET AS I WALK DOWNSTAIRS
OK
STEP
OW! RUFUS!
WHY ARE YOU LIKE THIS??
THE ONLY CONSTANT IN MY LIFE HAS BEEN YOU AND YOU'RE CRAZY
WOW. TOUCHÉ.

I WENT WILD SWIMMING AGAIN! THIS TIME WITH MY PALS JENI AND JODY.

IT WAS RAINING BUT THAT MADE IT ALL THE MORE FUN!

I HOPE THERE'S A THUNDER STORM!

IT FELT VERY PEACEFUL.

MY GOLDEN WAGTAIL EVEN CAME TO SEE ME!

SO NICE OF YOU TO DROP BY!

I'M ACTUALLY JUST HERE FOR THE FLIES.

I FOUND BISCUITS!
OH NICE!
HOLD UP... I THINK I BOUGHT THOSE AT CHRISTMAS...
WHAT'S THE SELL-BY DATE?
"BEST BEFORE... MARCH 2020"
SIGH
WASN'T EVERYTHING?

THE CAFE THAT I WORK IN PART TIME IS OPENING ON THE 15th JULY.
EMAIL FROM BOSS
ON THE ONE HAND IT WILL BE SO AMAZING TO SEE MY PALS AND CUSTOMERS AGAIN!
ON THE OTHER HAND I'M NOT SURE I'M GOING TO BE READY... I STILL HAVE PANIC ATTACKS GOING TO THE SUPERMARKET...
YOU'RE OBVIOUSLY NOT READY. TELL YOUR BOSS NOW AND THEN THEY'LL HAVE TIME TO GIVE YOUR SHIFTS-
TAKE A NAP AND WORRY ABOUT THIS TOMORROW
AND SO:

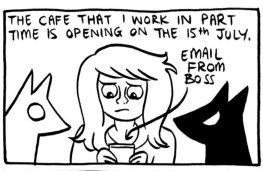

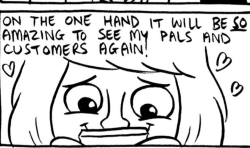

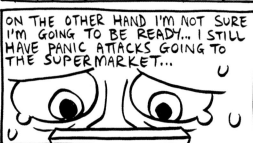

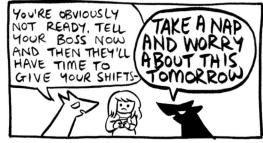

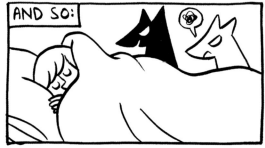

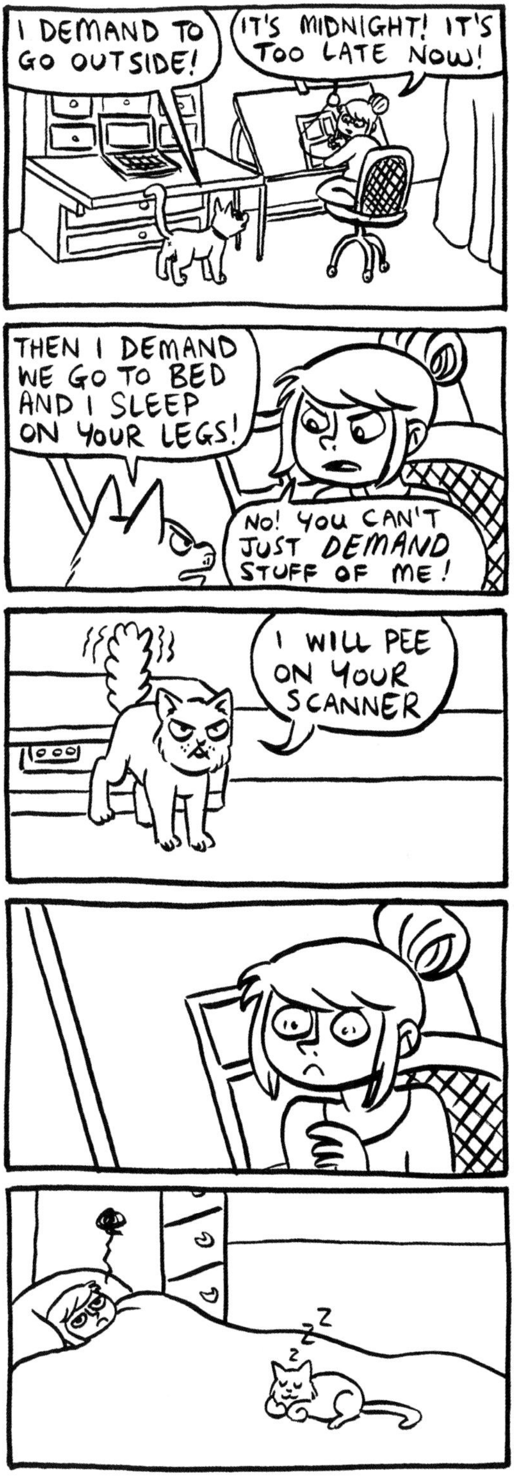
I DEMAND TO GO OUTSIDE!
IT'S MIDNIGHT! IT'S TOO LATE NOW!
THEN I DEMAND WE GO TO BED AND I SLEEP ON YOUR LEGS!
NO! YOU CAN'T JUST DEMAND STUFF OF ME!
I WILL PEE ON YOUR SCANNER
Z Z Z

MY HOUSEMATE IAIN HAS BOUGHT A HOUSE, SO HE'LL BE MOVING OUT SOON.
I DON'T KNOW WHAT THAT MEANS FOR ME JUST YET.
BARKY HAS (OF COURSE) TAKEN THIS OPPORTUNITY TO BE A DICK.
NO ONE ELSE IS GOING TO WANT TO LIVE WITH YOU.
IT'S BEEN A LITTLE TOUGH.
NOT EVEN YOU WANT TO LIVE WITH YOU. BUT YOU HAVE NO CHOICE.
HEH HEH!
THANK GOODNESS FOR FRIENDLY.
WHENEVER YOU'RE READY, I'LL HELP YOU GO THROUGH YOUR OPTIONS.

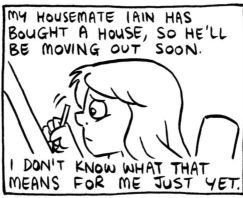

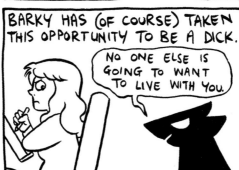

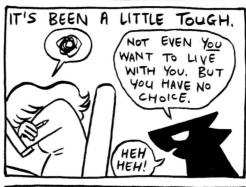

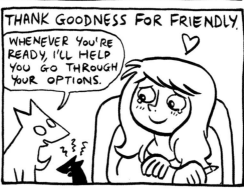

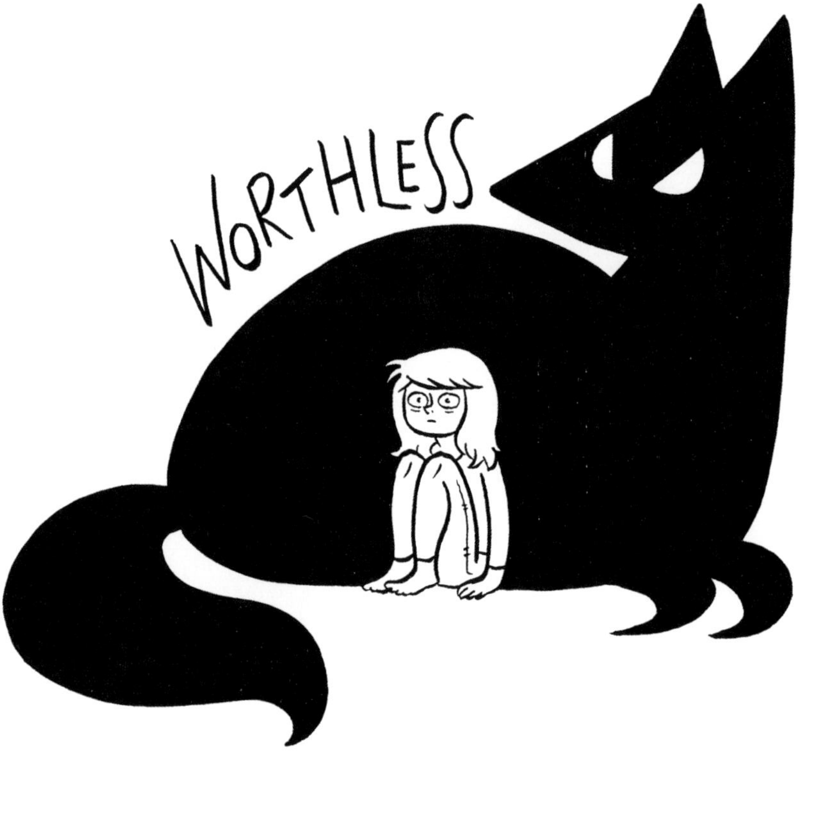
WORTHLESS

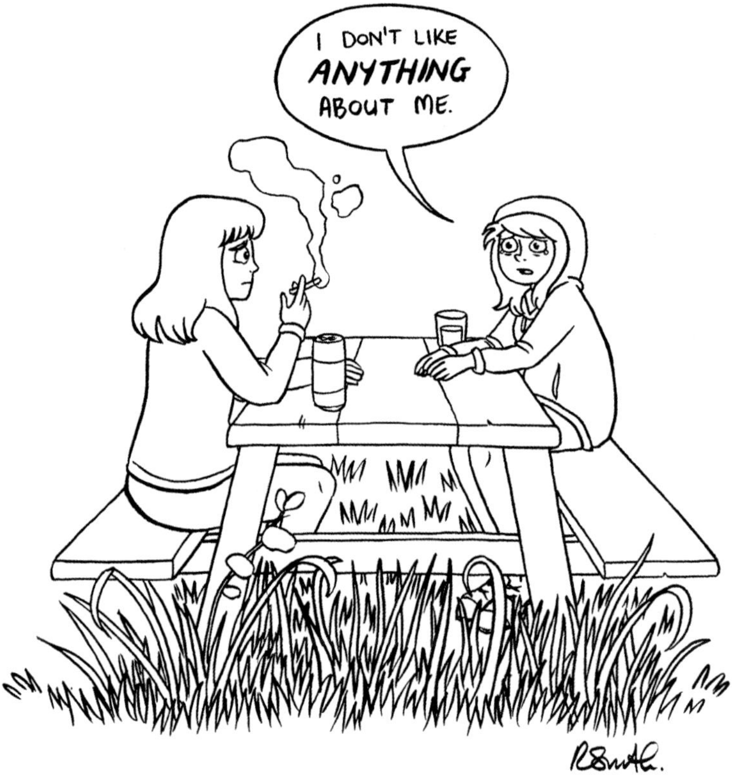
I DON'T LIKE ANYTHING ABOUT ME.

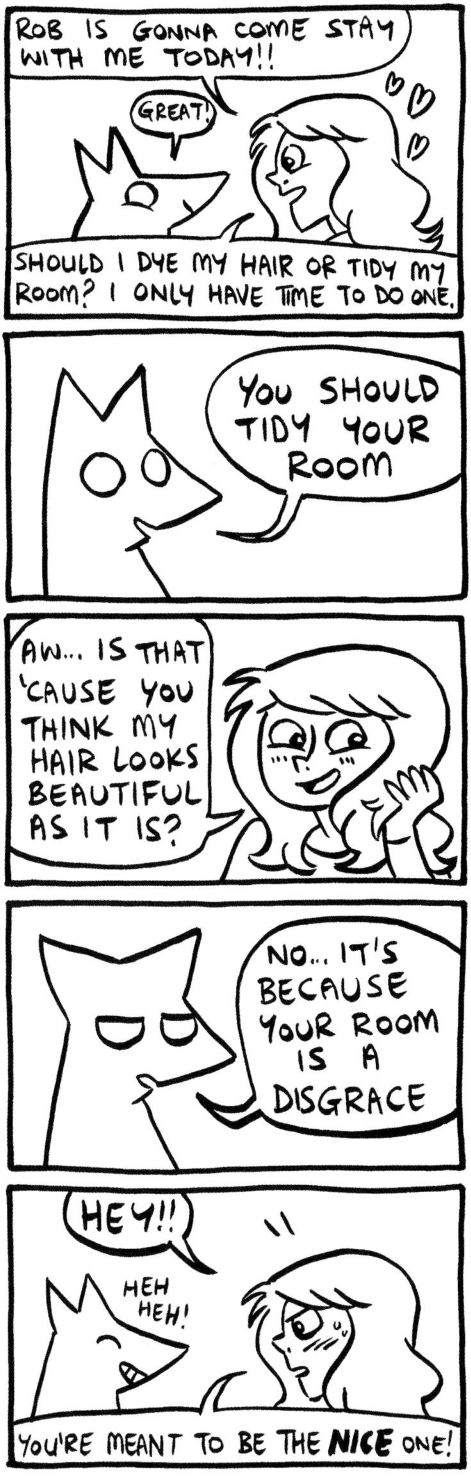
ROB IS GONNA COME STAY WITH ME TODAY!!
GREAT!
SHOULD I DYE MY HAIR OR TIDY MY ROOM? I ONLY HAVE TIME TO DO ONE.
YOU SHOULD TIDY YOUR ROOM
AW... IS THAT 'CAUSE YOU THINK MY HAIR LOOKS BEAUTIFUL AS IT IS?
NO... IT'S BECAUSE YOUR ROOM IS A DISGRACE
HEY!!
HEH HEH!
YOU'RE MEANT TO BE THE NICE ONE!

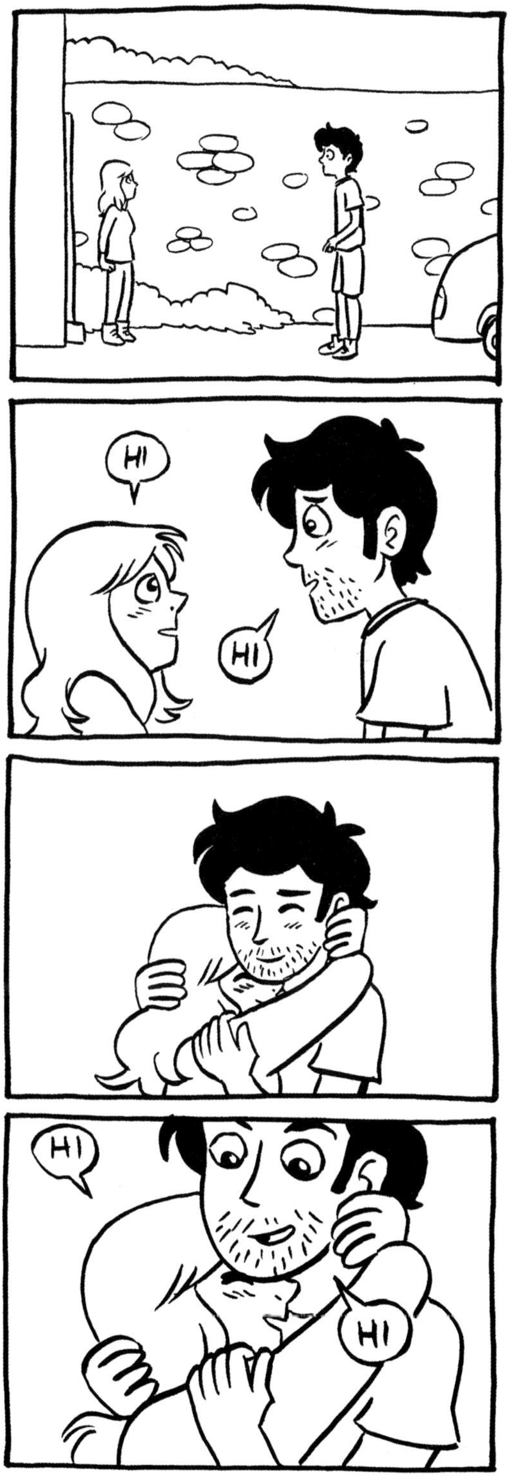
HI
HI
HI
HI

I THINK I NEED TO PUT ANOTHER HOLE IN MY BELT...
AW BABE...
I THINK EVERYONE HAS PUT ON A BIT OF WEIGHT DURING LOCKDOWN ... I KNOW I HAVE...
NO... I MEAN...THE OTHER WAY AROUND ...MY SHORTS KEEP FALLING DOWN...
...
ARE YOU KIDDING ME!!? YOU ARE ALWAYS EATING!!
POKE POKE
HA! SORRY!

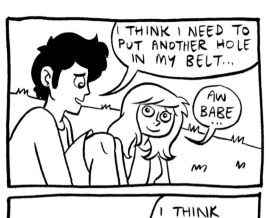

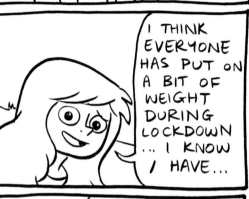

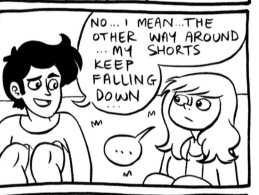

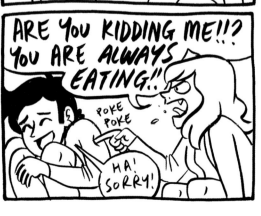

WAITING IN LINE FOR THE POST OFFICE...
ME
IT'S SO WEIRD RIGHT NOW, RIGHT?
OH I KNOW! ALL THESE MASKS!
TELL ME ABOUT IT!
I WALKED THROUGH TOWN TODAY AND IT FELT NORMAL! ... THEN THREE PEOPLE WALKED BY WITH MASKS ON AND RUINED IT!
SUCH A SHAME
WOAH! I JUST NEARLY LOST MY EYES BY ROLLING THEM TOO HARD!

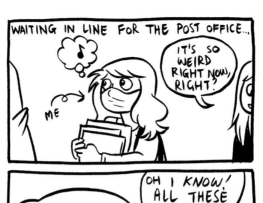

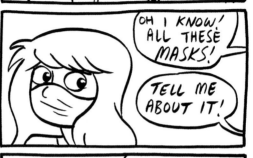

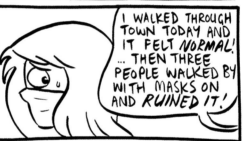

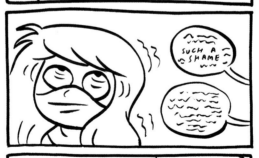

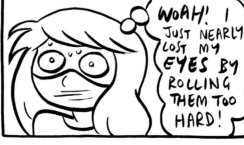

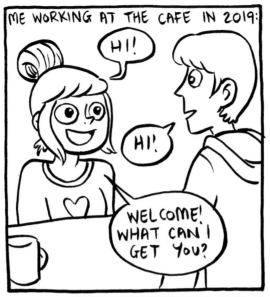

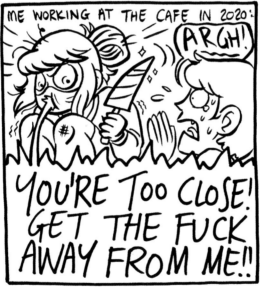

ME WORKING AT THE CAFE IN 2019:
HI!
HI!
WELCOME! WHAT CAN I GET YOU?
ME WORKING AT THE CAFE IN 2020:
ARGH!
YOU'RE TOO CLOSE! GET THE FUCK AWAY FROM ME!!
SO YEAH... I'VE DECIDED NOT TO GO BACK TO MY PART-TIME JOB UNTIL WE HAVE A VACCINE ON ACCOUNT OF ME PROBABLY STABBING A CUSTOMER IN THE FACE WHEN THEY GET TOO CLOSE.

RACHEL
ME
THERE'S NO WAY THEY'RE ALL IN THE SAME HOUSEHOLD
WHEN DID TEENS GET SO *HOT*??
WHEN *I* WAS A TEEN I LIVED IN HUGE NEON TRACKSUITS THAT USED TO BELONG TO MY BROTHERS
I DON'T THINK I REALIZED I HAD A *BODY* UNTIL I WAS 20!
HA HA!

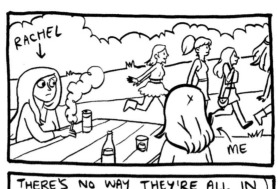

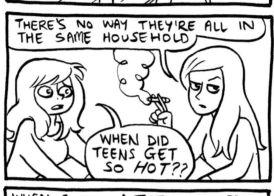

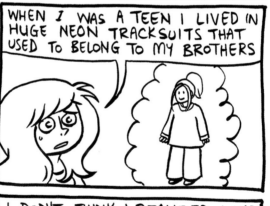

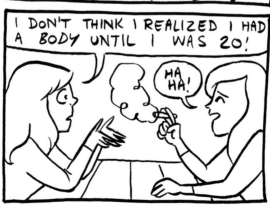

I MISS PUBS SO MUCH...
YE OLDE PUB
BUT THERE'S NO WAY I'M GOING IN THERE...

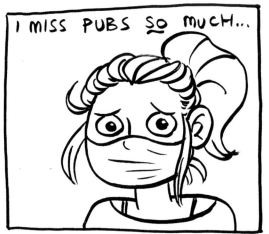

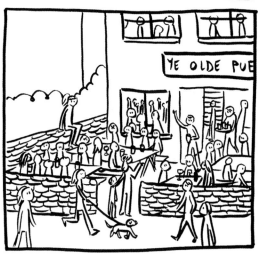

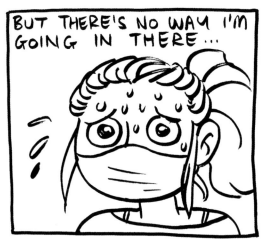

HOME IS
WHEREVER I'M
WITH
YOU.

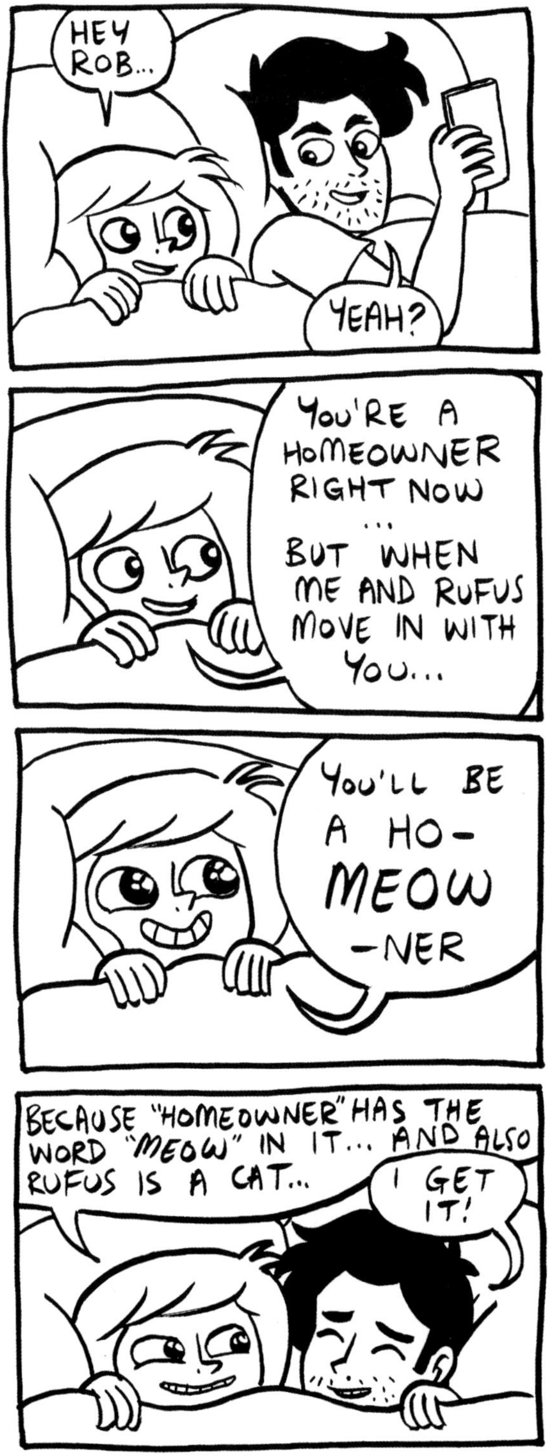
HEY ROB...
YEAH?
YOU'RE A HOMEOWNER RIGHT NOW ... BUT WHEN ME AND RUFUS MOVE IN WITH YOU...
YOU'LL BE A HO-MEOW-NER
BECAUSE "HOMEOWNER" HAS THE WORD "MEOW" IN IT... AND ALSO RUFUS IS A CAT...
I GET IT!

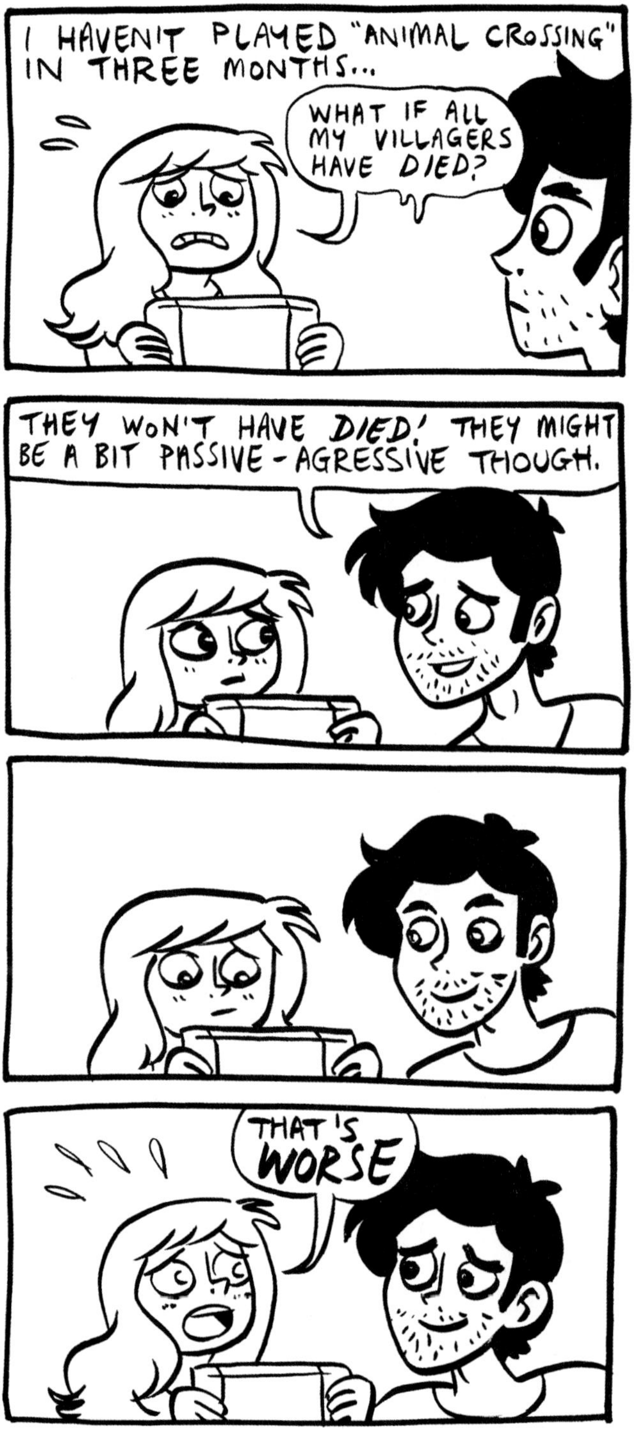

I HAVEN'T PLAYED "ANIMAL CROSSING" IN THREE MONTHS...
WHAT IF ALL MY VILLAGERS HAVE DIED?
THEY WON'T HAVE DIED! THEY MIGHT BE A BIT PASSIVE-AGRESSIVE THOUGH.
THAT'S WORSE

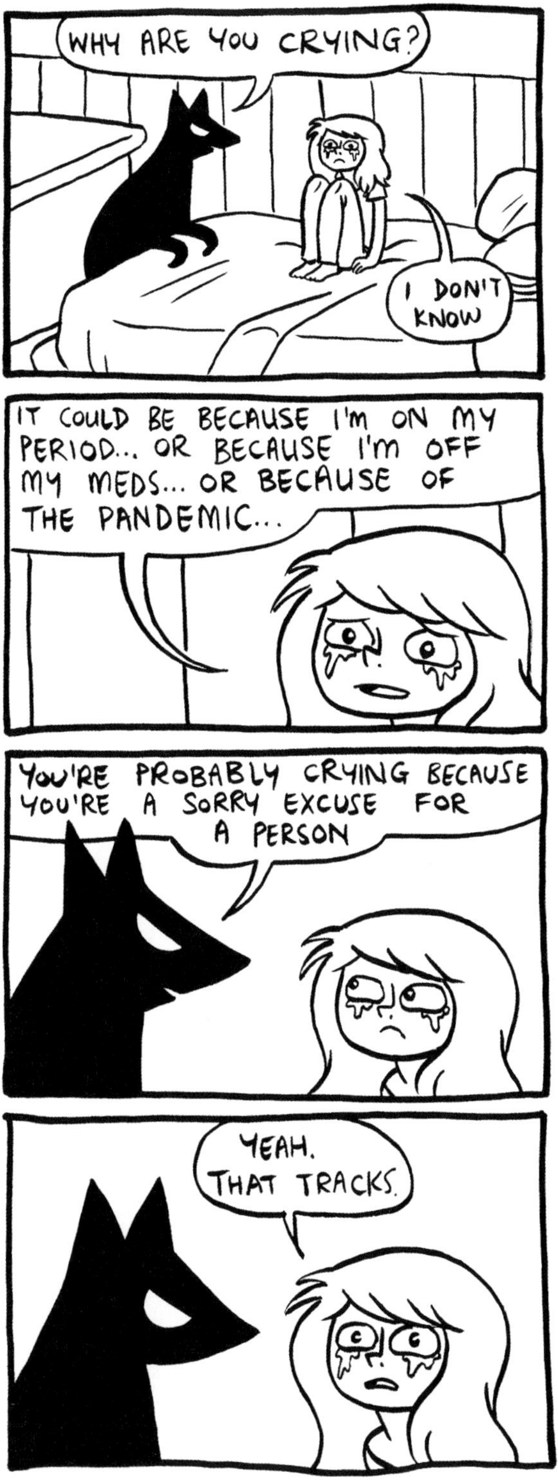
WHY ARE YOU CRYING?
I DON'T KNOW
IT COULD BE BECAUSE I'M ON MY PERIOD... OR BECAUSE I'M OFF MY MEDS... OR BECAUSE OF THE PANDEMIC...
YOU'RE PROBABLY CRYING BECAUSE YOU'RE A SORRY EXCUSE FOR A PERSON
YEAH. THAT TRACKS.

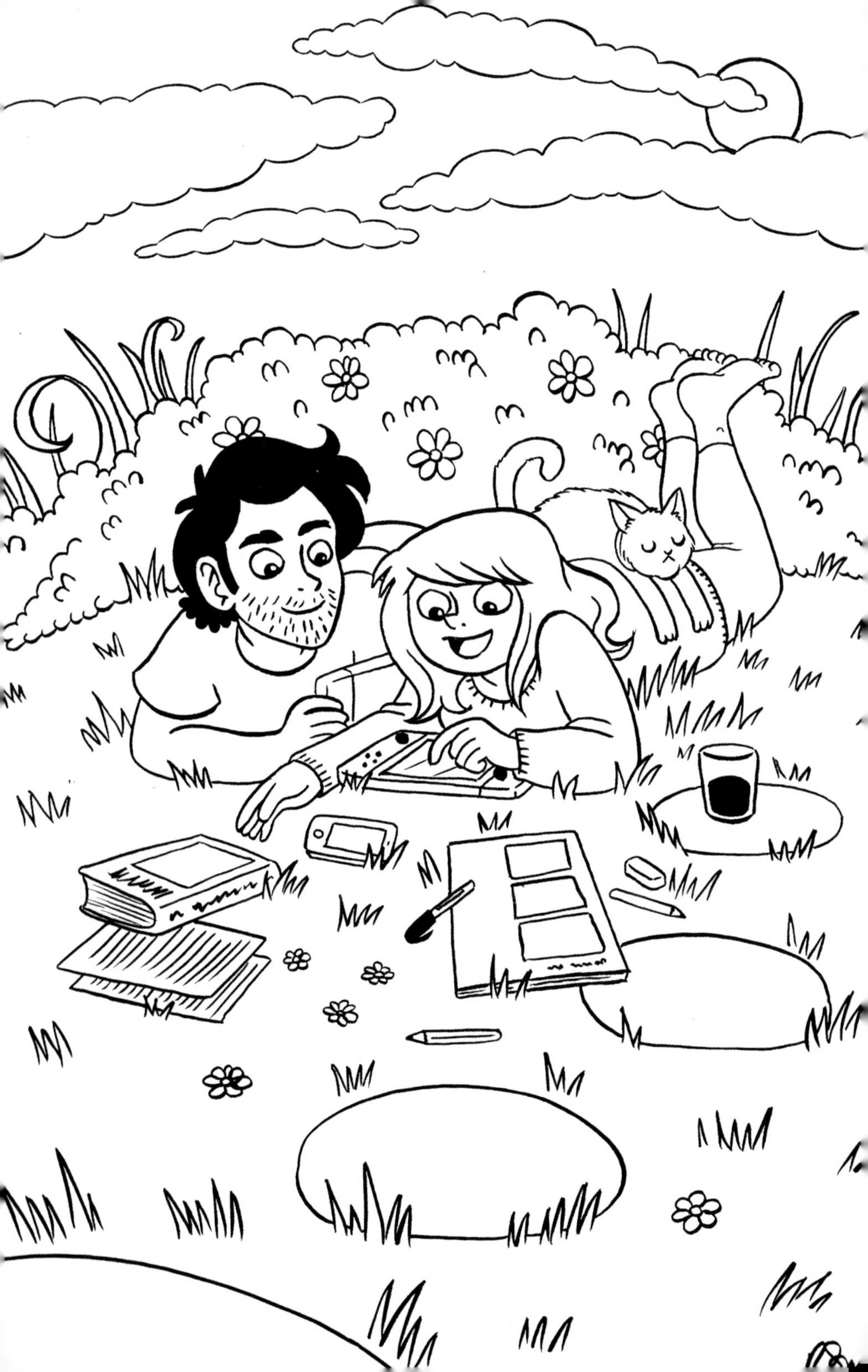

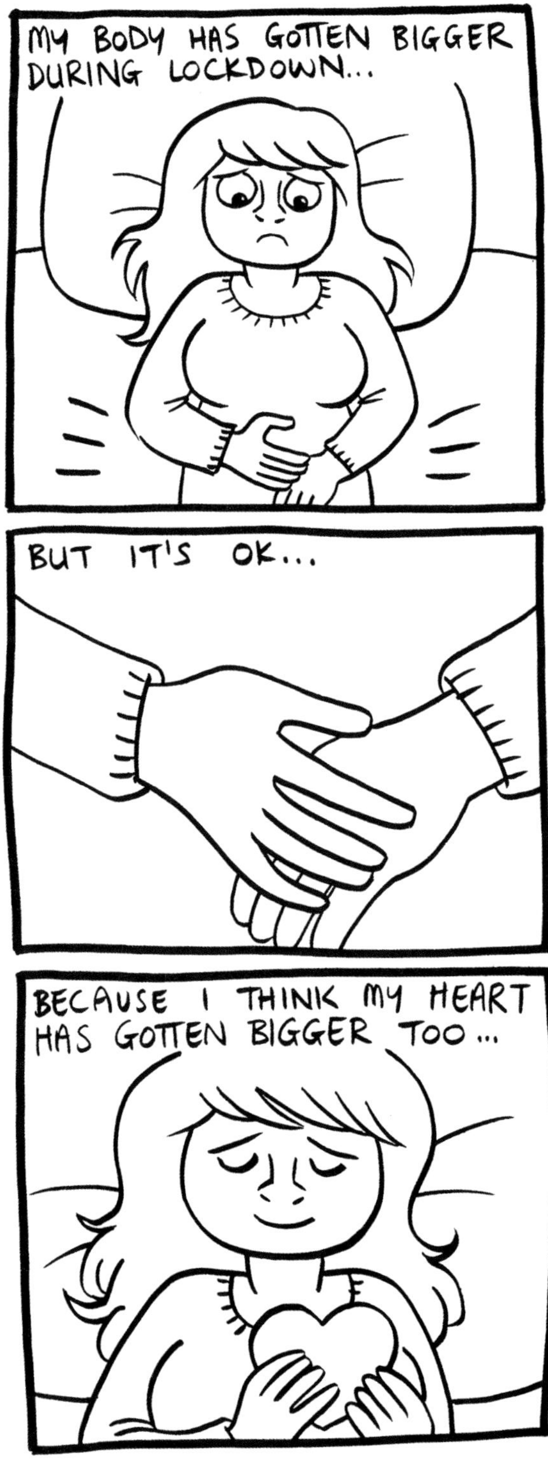
MY BODY HAS GOTTEN BIGGER DURING LOCKDOWN...
BUT IT'S OK...
BECAUSE I THINK MY HEART HAS GOTTEN BIGGER TOO...

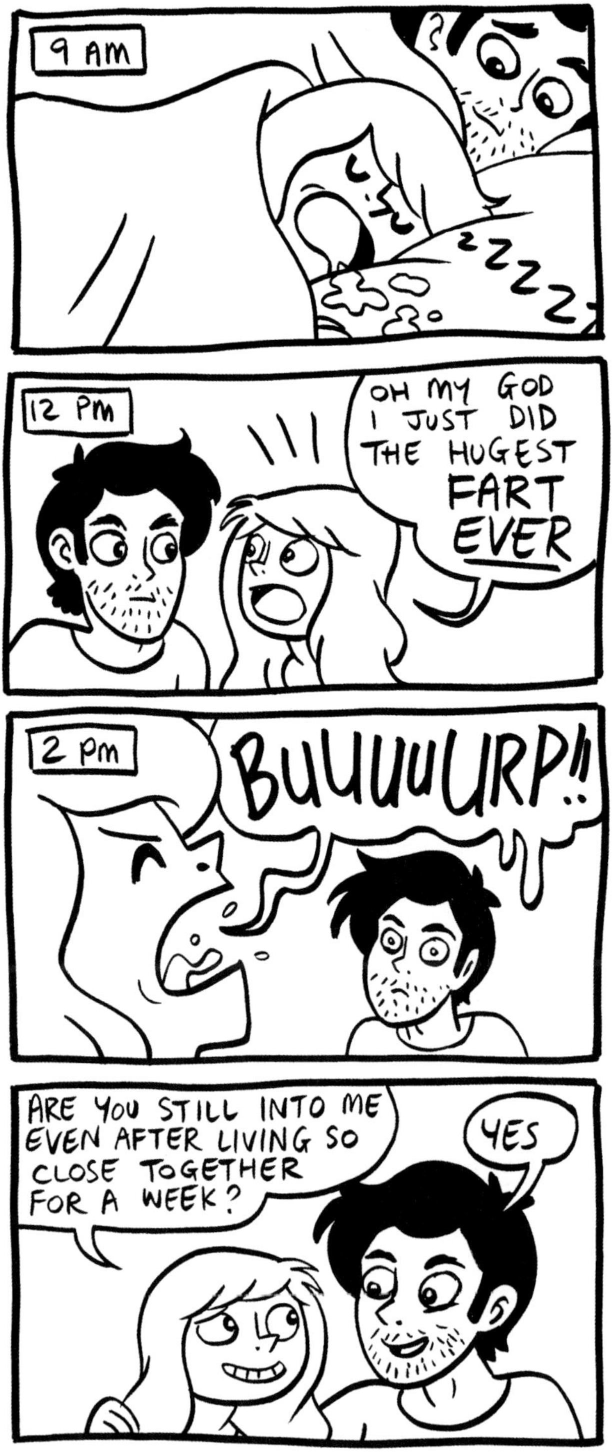
9 AM
ZZZZZ
12 PM
OH MY GOD I JUST DID THE HUGEST FART EVER
2 pm
BUUUUURP!!
ARE YOU STILL INTO ME EVEN AFTER LIVING SO CLOSE TOGETHER FOR A WEEK?
YES

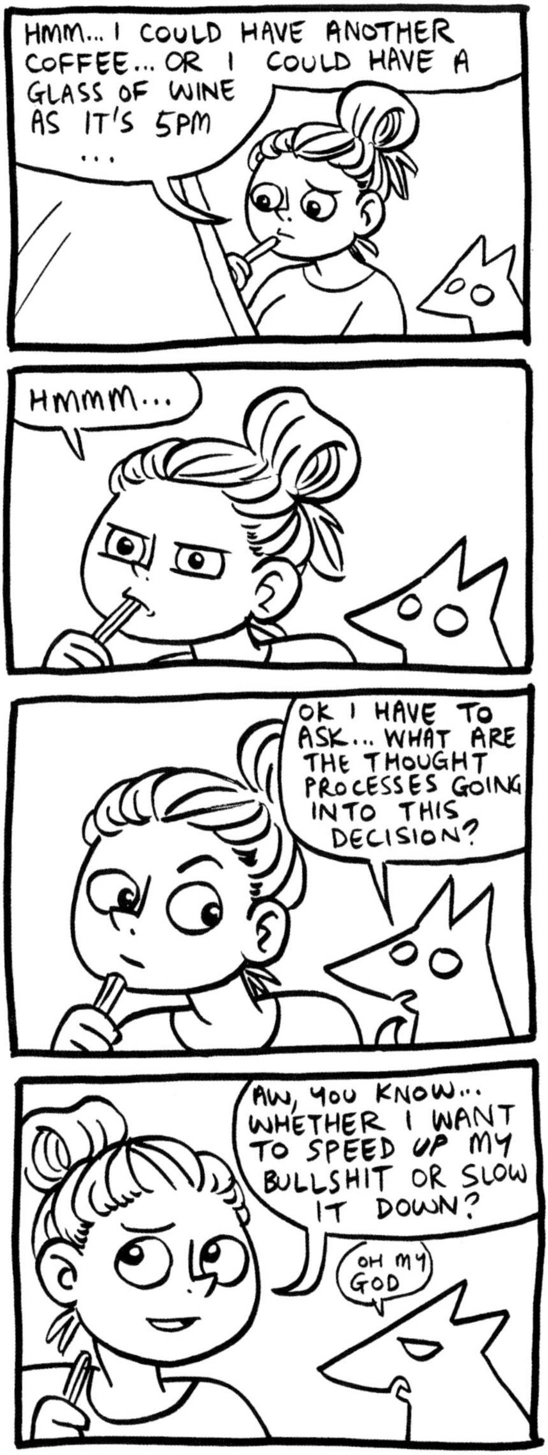
HMM... I COULD HAVE ANOTHER COFFEE... OR I COULD HAVE A GLASS OF WINE AS IT'S 5PM ...
HMMM...
OK I HAVE TO ASK... WHAT ARE THE THOUGHT PROCESSES GOING INTO THIS DECISION?
AW, YOU KNOW... WHETHER I WANT TO SPEED UP MY BULLSHIT OR SLOW IT DOWN?
OH MY GOD

A COMPANY I'VE BEEN WORKING WITH HAVEN'T BEEN TREATING ME VERY WELL... I DECIDED TO STICK UP FOR MYSELF AND EMAIL THEM VERY POLITELY...
HI, UM... YOU TOOK MY EDITOR AWAY AND I HAVEN'T HEARD FROM YOU IN OVER A YEAR...
TAP TAP TAP
IMMEDIATELY AFTER I HIT SEND I FELT HUGE REGRET...
WHO THE FUCK DO I THINK I AM?
EVEN THOUGH I HAVE SO MUCH WORK TO DO...
FOLLOW
I HAVE TO GO TO BED FOR A WHILE WITH A BRAIN FULL OF IMPOSTER SYNDROME.
YOU SHOULD FEEL LUCKY THAT ANYONE WANTS TO WORK WITH YOU!

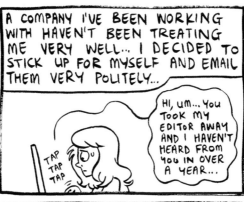

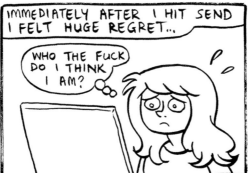

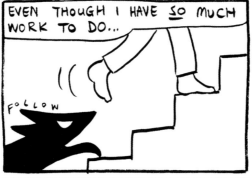

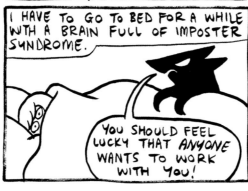

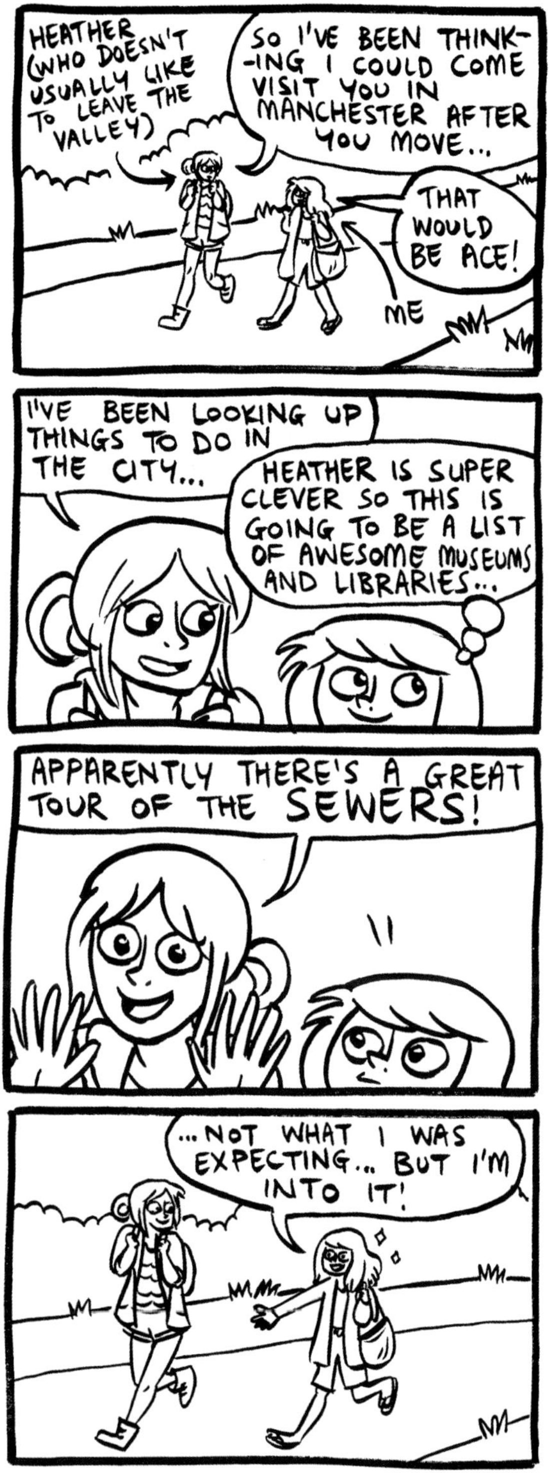
HEATHER (WHO DOESN'T USUALLY LIKE TO LEAVE THE VALLEY)
SO I'VE BEEN THINK-ING I COULD COME VISIT YOU IN MANCHESTER AFTER YOU MOVE...
THAT WOULD BE ACE!
ME
I'VE BEEN LOOKING UP THINGS TO DO IN THE CITY...
HEATHER IS SUPER CLEVER SO THIS IS GOING TO BE A LIST OF AWESOME MUSEUMS AND LIBRARIES...
APPARENTLY THERE'S A GREAT TOUR OF THE SEWERS!
...NOT WHAT I WAS EXPECTING... BUT I'M INTO IT!

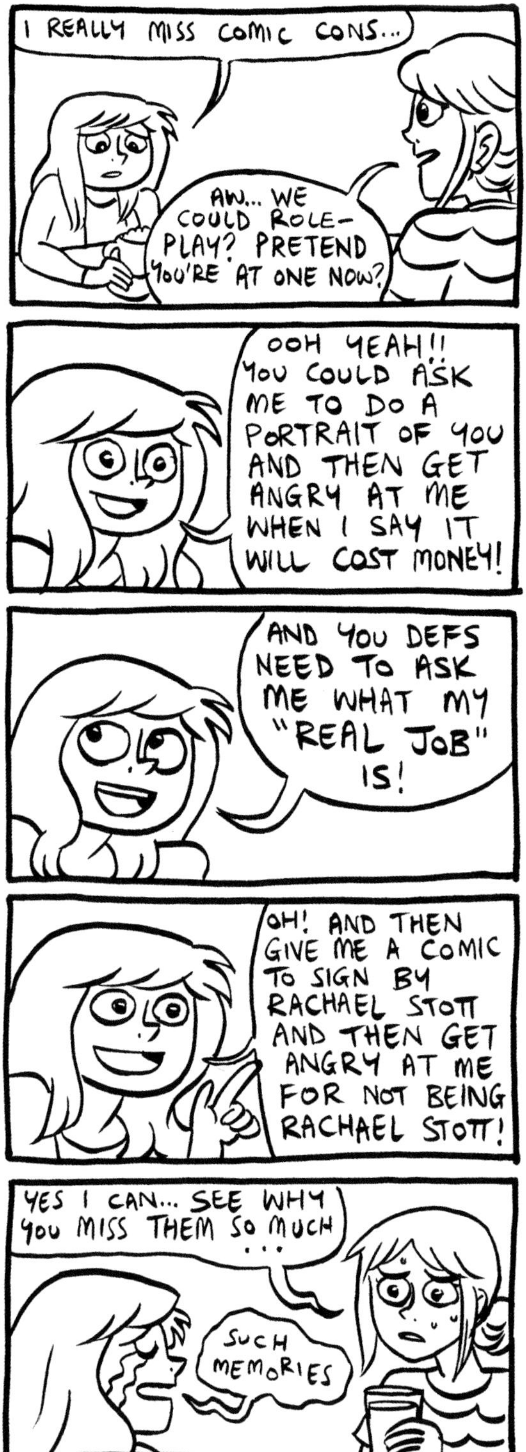
I REALLY MISS COMIC CONS...
AW... WE COULD ROLE-PLAY? PRETEND YOU'RE AT ONE NOW?
OOH YEAH!! YOU COULD ASK ME TO DO A PORTRAIT OF YOU AND THEN GET ANGRY AT ME WHEN I SAY IT WILL COST MONEY!
AND YOU DEFS NEED TO ASK ME WHAT MY "REAL JOB" IS!
OH! AND THEN GIVE ME A COMIC TO SIGN BY RACHAEL STOTT AND THEN GET ANGRY AT ME FOR NOT BEING RACHAEL STOTT!
YES I CAN... SEE WHY YOU MISS THEM SO MUCH ...
SUCH MEMORIES

SINCE THE PANDEMIC STARTED I'VE BEEN HAVING REALLY AWFUL ANXIETY DREAMS...
GASP PANT... PANT... PANT...
JUST A DREAM...
JUST A DREAM...
BUT EVERY NOW AND AGAIN...
I'LL HAVE A REALLY GOOD DREAM TO MAKE UP FOR THE BAD ONES.
I DREAMT ABOUT MY ALOE VERA PLANT!
SHE TOLD ME SHE WANTED TO BE A DETECTIVE!
COOL! DID SHE SOLVE ANY CRIMES...?
NO... WE SPENT THE WHOLE DREAM FINDING HER A COOL HAT!

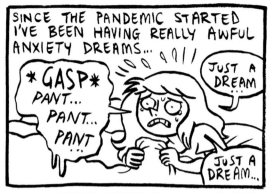

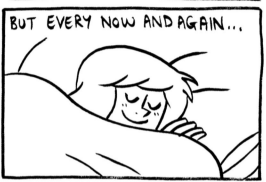

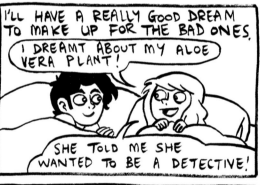

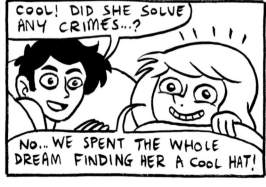

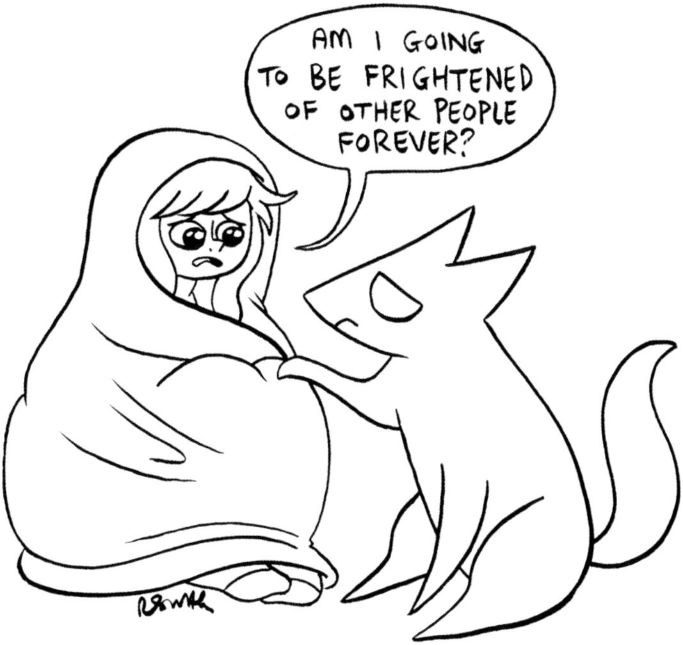
AM I GOING TO BE FRIGHTENED OF OTHER PEOPLE FOREVER?

HELLO!
HEY! THAT IS A SHIRT I'VE NOT SEEN!
A VERY YELLOW SHIRT
HAHA! DOES IT LOOK SILLY?
NO! I LIKE IT!
YOU LOOK LIKE A REFEREE!
I WAS GONNA GO FOR A RUN...
OOH! TAKE SOME RED CARDS AND HAND THEM TO PEOPLE NOT WEARING MASKS!

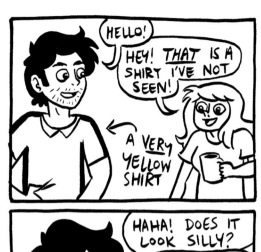

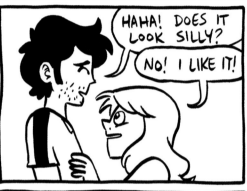

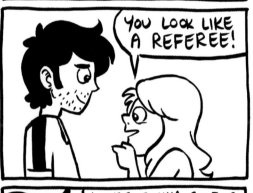

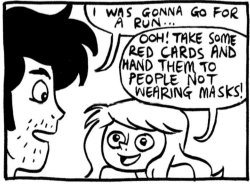

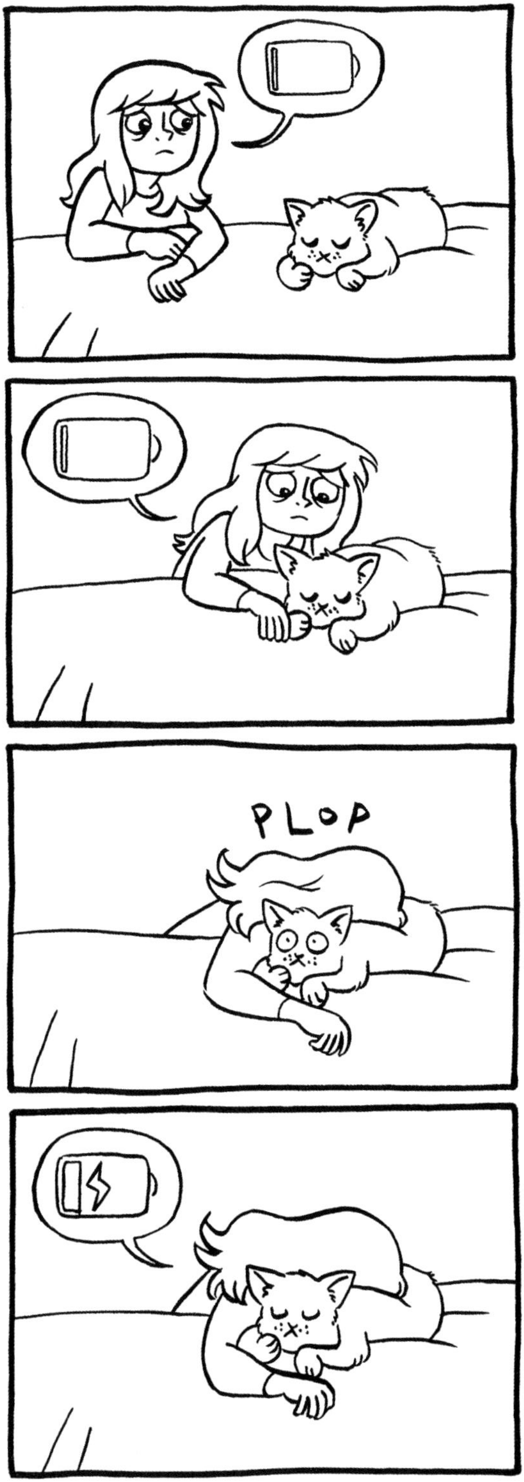
PLOP

THINGS FEEL LIKE THEY'RE LOOKING UP! I JUST HAD A REAL LOVELY PHONE MEETING WITH MY AGENT...
AND THINGS SEEM TO BE GOING BACK TO NORMAL! I'M GONNA GO BACK TO WORK NEXT WEEK AND SEE MY NANA IN A COUPLE OF DAYS...
UM... NO... I'VE NOT SEEN THE NEWS...
WELL
FUCK

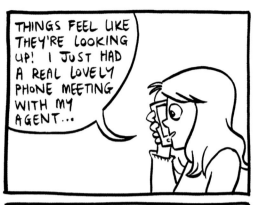

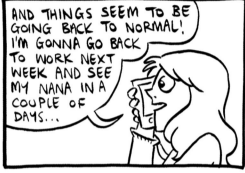

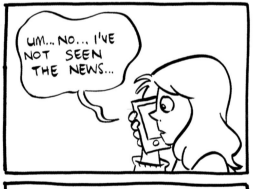

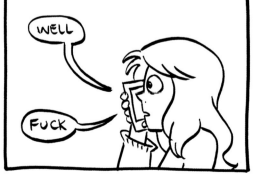

READING ABOUT THE NEW LOCKDOWN RULES FOR THE NORTH OF ENGLAND...
SO I CAN'T HAVE A PAL COME SIT IN MY GARDEN... BUT WE CAN GO TO A BUSY BEER GARDEN ...
I CAN'T LET A PAL INSIDE MY HOUSE ... BUT WE CAN GO INSIDE BUSY CAFES AND RESTAURANTS ...
THIS MAKES NO SENSE!
BASICALLY YOU CAN'T SEE ANY- -ONE OR DO ANYTHING UNLESS YOU HAVE TO SPEND MONEY
YEAH... THAT TRACKS

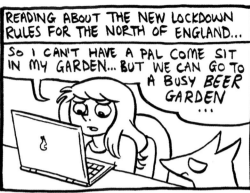

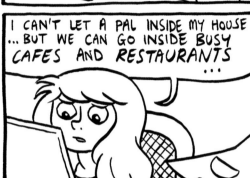

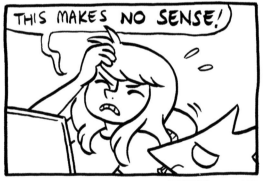

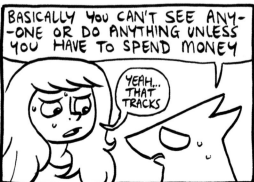

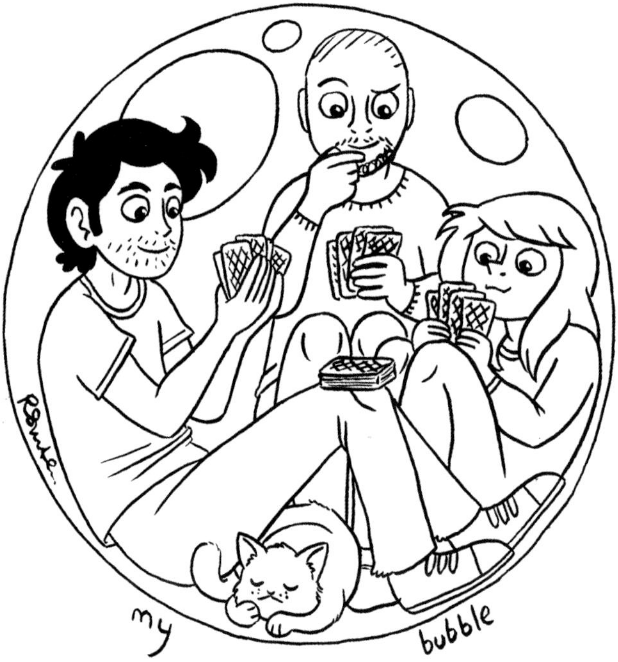
my
bubble

MY NANA IS ILL. SHE MIGHT HAVE TO GO TO A CARE HOME SOON. PERMANENTLY.
I CAN'T GO TO SEE HER, DUE TO THE NEW LOCKDOWN RULES. I COULD BREAK THE RULES...BUT IF I GAVE SOMETHING TO NANA...
I SIMPLY COULD NOT LIVE WITH MYSELF...
THIS ISN'T EXACTLY A HOT TAKE ...
BUT THIS PANDEMIC FUCKING SUCKS ASS

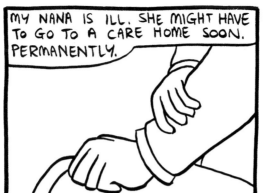

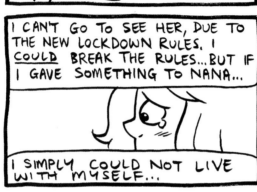

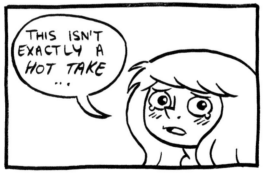

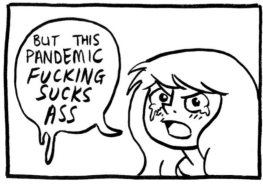

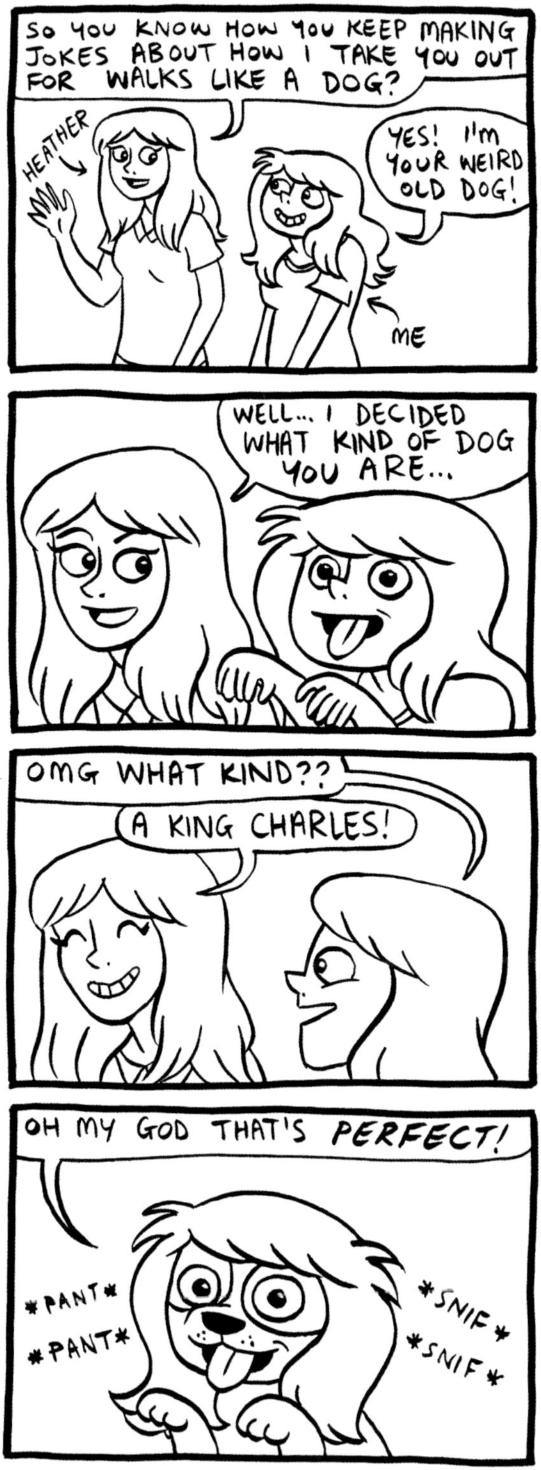
SO YOU KNOW HOW YOU KEEP MAKING JOKES ABOUT HOW I TAKE YOU OUT FOR WALKS LIKE A DOG?
HEATHER
YES! I'M YOUR WEIRD OLD DOG!
ME
WELL... I DECIDED WHAT KIND OF DOG YOU ARE...
OMG WHAT KIND??
A KING CHARLES!
OH MY GOD THAT'S PERFECT!
PANT
PANT
SNIF
SNIF

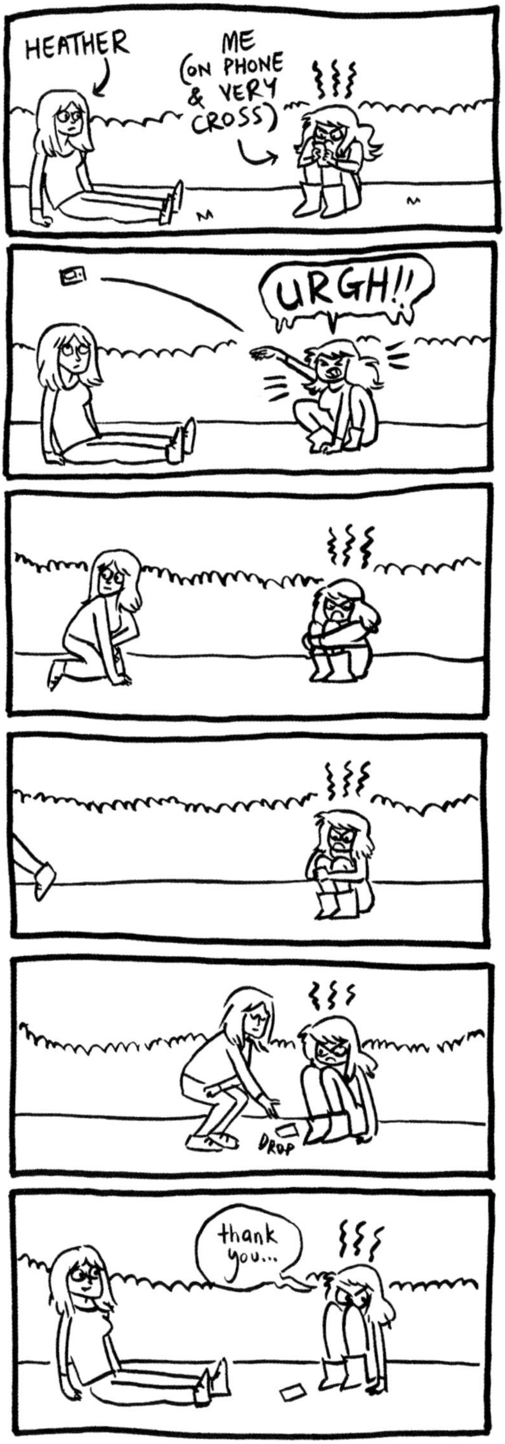
HEATHER
ME (ON PHONE & VERY CROSS)
URGH!!
DROP
thank you...

♪!
♪!
♪!
♪ SHINY, SHINY, SHINY BOOTS OF LEATHER...♪
...DOWNY SINS OF STREETLIGHT FANCIES CHASE THE COSTUMES SHE SHALL WEAR... ERMINE FURS...ADORN THE IMPERIOUS... SEVERIN, SEVERIN AWAITS YOU THERE...
HMM
I AM TIRED, I AM WEARY, I COULD SLEEP FOR A THOUSAND YEARS

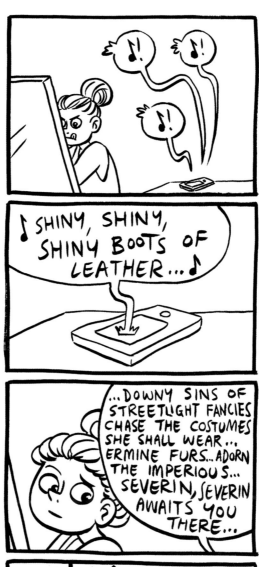

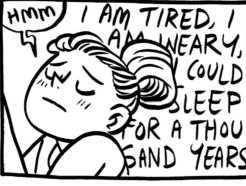

14 YEARS AGO, ON AUGUST 8th, TWO POLICE OFFICERS CAME TO MY HOUSE TO TELL ME MY DAD HAD PASSED AWAY.
I KNOW IT'S JUST A DATE, AND THERE'S NO REASON I SHOULD MISS HIM MORE ON AUGUST 8th THAN ANY OTHER DAY... BUT I ALWAYS FEEL A BIT LOST.
INSTEAD OF THINKING ABOUT HIS DEATH, WHY NOT CELEBRATE HIS *LIFE*?
DON'T I DO THAT EVERY DAY JUST BY EXISTING?
THAT'S A LOVELY THOUGHT. HE WOULD BE VERY PROUD OF YOU.
SIGH

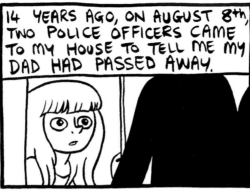

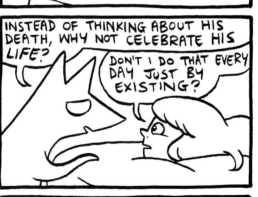

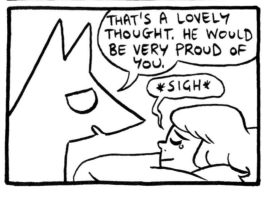

SINCE THE PANDEMIC I'VE FELT MY ENERGY TAKE A NOSEDIVE...

THIS WEEK IT'S GOT A BIT WORSE...

I FEEL LIKE A LITTLE PAT OF BUTTER...

...THAT HAS BEEN SPREAD OVER TOO MANY PIECES OF TOAST.

MAYBE I NEED TO CHOOSE MY PIECES OF TOAST MORE CARE— —FULLY...

I FINALLY FELT SAFE ENOUGH TO GO BACK TO MY PART-TIME CAFE JOB.

IT FELT VERY STRANGE, BUT SO SO GOOD TO SEE EVERYONE!

YAY! WE'RE ON SHIFT TOGETHER!

YAAY!

KATIE

AFTER FIVE MONTHS OFF, SOME THINGS CAME STRAIGHT BACK TO ME!

(PERFECT MILK FOAM ON A CAPPUCINO)

AW YEAH

AAAND SOME THINGS DIDN'T...

KATIE?

HOW DO I OPEN THE TILL??

REALLY?

NEEDS TO GO THIS WAY
PLENTY O' ROOM TO GO THROUGH ERE', LOVE
(WHAT I THOUGHT WAS) A FRIENDLY WAVE AND SMILE
WE'VE NOT GOT FLEAS, BITCH!!
WTF

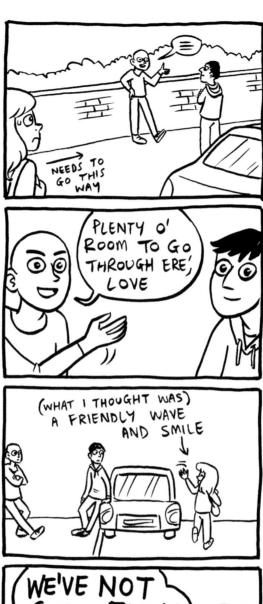

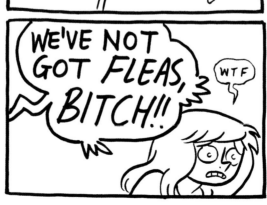

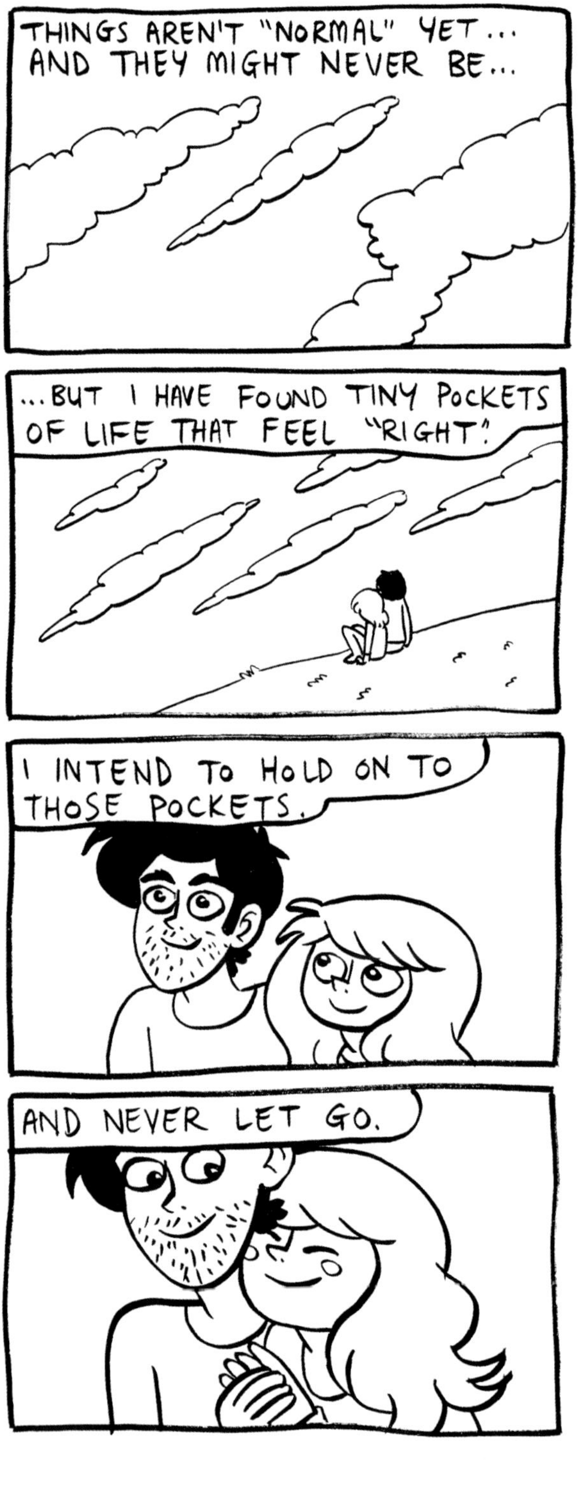
THINGS AREN'T "NORMAL" YET... AND THEY MIGHT NEVER BE...
...BUT I HAVE FOUND TINY POCKETS OF LIFE THAT FEEL "RIGHT".
I INTEND TO HOLD ON TO THOSE POCKETS.
AND NEVER LET GO.

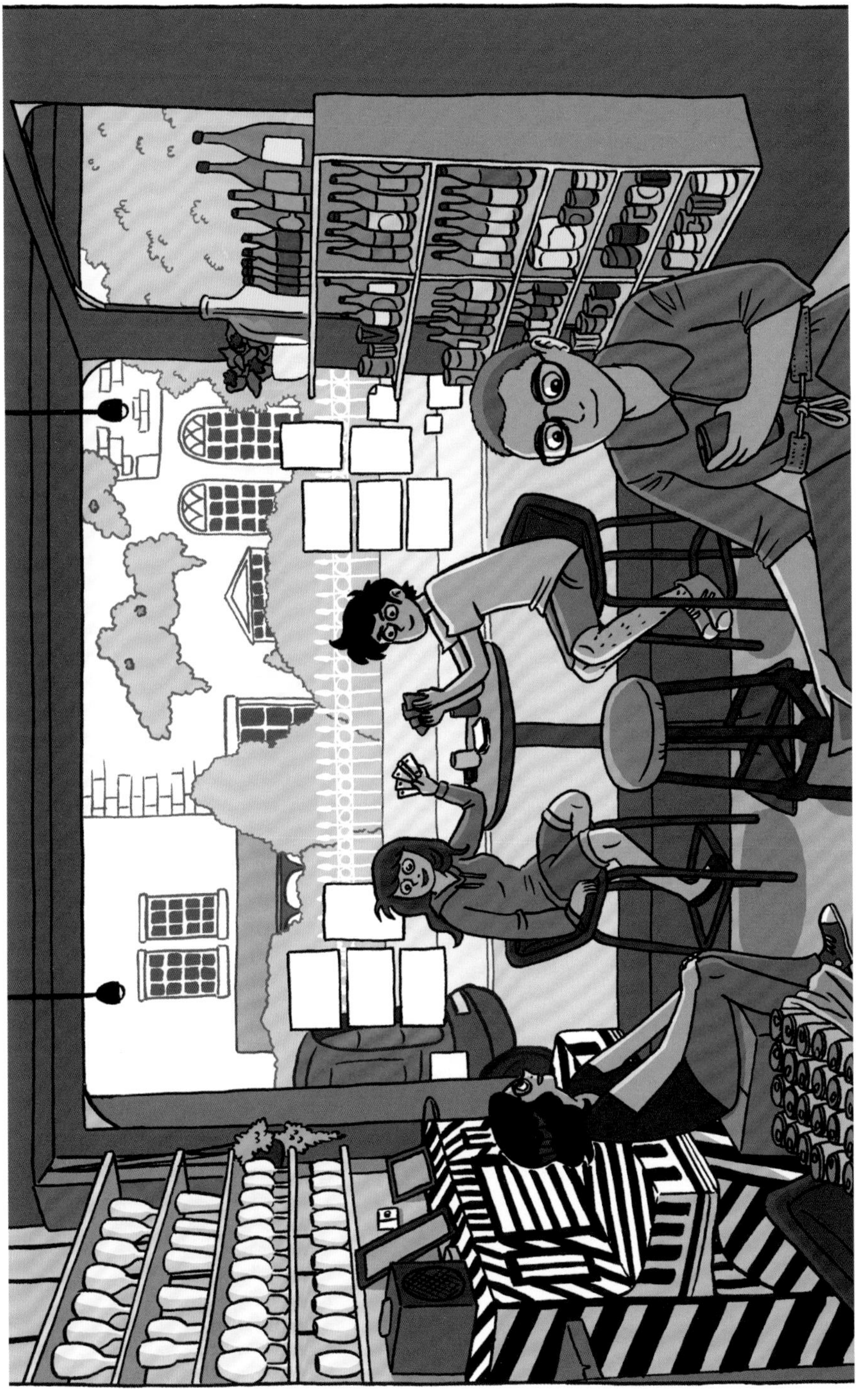

EPILOGUE....

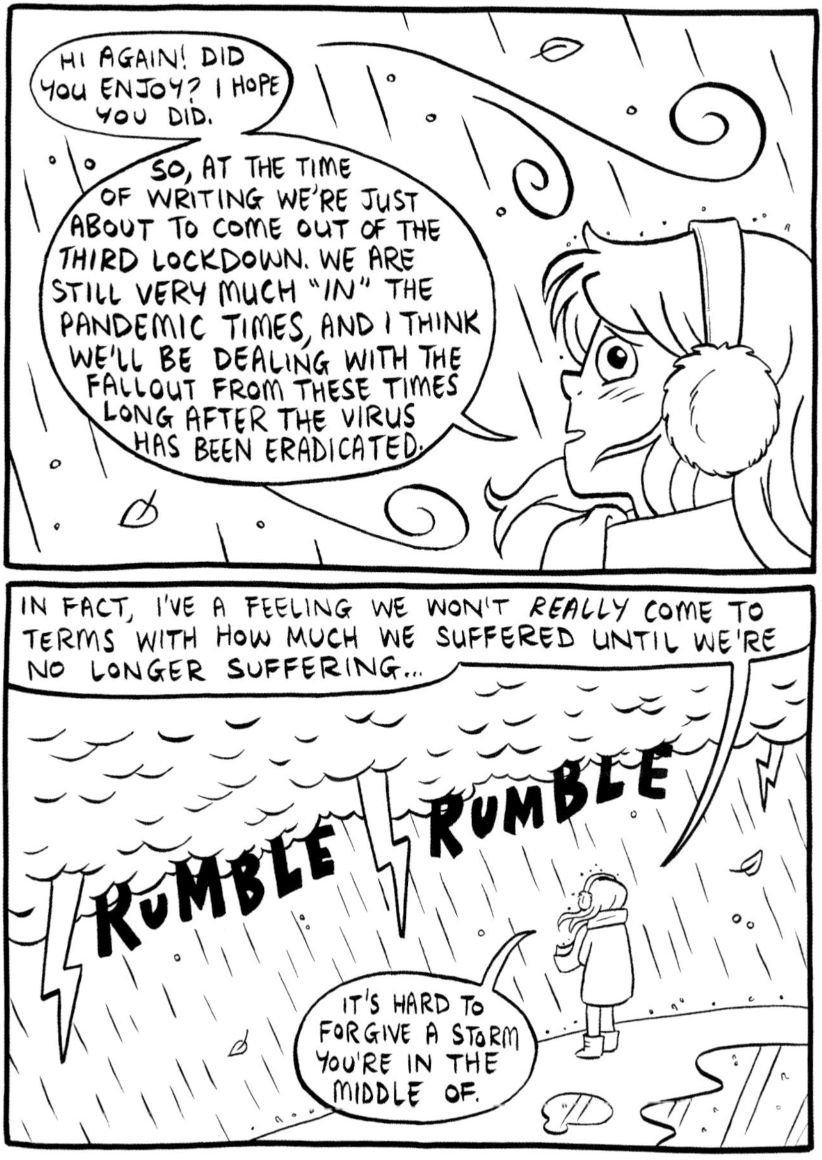
HI AGAIN! DID YOU ENJOY? I HOPE YOU DID.
SO, AT THE TIME OF WRITING WE'RE JUST ABOUT TO COME OUT OF THE THIRD LOCKDOWN. WE ARE STILL VERY MUCH "IN" THE PANDEMIC TIMES, AND I THINK WE'LL BE DEALING WITH THE FALLOUT FROM THESE TIMES LONG AFTER THE VIRUS HAS BEEN ERADICATED.
IN FACT, I'VE A FEELING WE WON'T *REALLY* COME TO TERMS WITH HOW MUCH WE SUFFERED UNTIL WE'RE NO LONGER SUFFERING...
RUMBLE
RUMBLE
IT'S HARD TO FORGIVE A STORM YOU'RE IN THE MIDDLE OF.

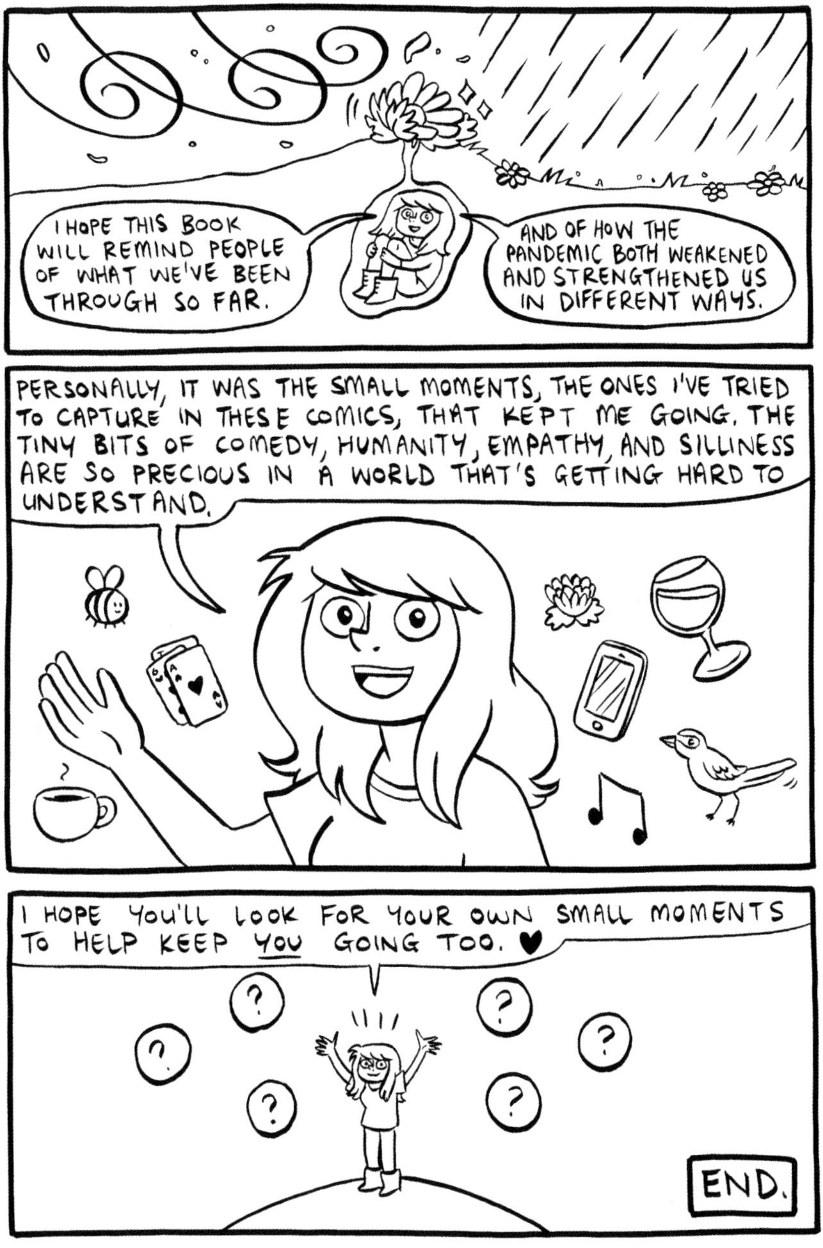
I HOPE THIS BOOK WILL REMIND PEOPLE OF WHAT WE'VE BEEN THROUGH SO FAR.
AND OF HOW THE PANDEMIC BOTH WEAKENED AND STRENGTHENED US IN DIFFERENT WAYS.
PERSONALLY, IT WAS THE SMALL MOMENTS, THE ONES I'VE TRIED TO CAPTURE IN THESE COMICS, THAT KEPT ME GOING. THE TINY BITS OF COMEDY, HUMANITY, EMPATHY, AND SILLINESS ARE SO PRECIOUS IN A WORLD THAT'S GETTING HARD TO UNDERSTAND.
I HOPE YOU'LL LOOK FOR YOUR OWN SMALL MOMENTS TO HELP KEEP YOU GOING TOO. ♥
END.

ABOUT THE AUTHOR

RACHAEL ♥

Rachael Smith is a UK-based comics creator whose
books include: **WIRED UP WRONG**, **STAND IN YOUR
POWER**, **ARTIFICIAL FLOWERS**, and **THE RABBIT**.
She usually writes something about her cat and her
boyfriend here but perhaps you don't need that
after reading 200 comics about how she lives.

Website: rachaelsmith.org
Twitter: @rachael_
Instagram: flimsy_kitten

ACKNOWLEDGEMENTS

Thank you to Heather, for giving me the idea to start documenting these strange times with these comics.

Thank you to everyone who I drew in these comics for letting me draw them in these comics.

Thank you to everyone who read these comics online, in particular the ones who told me I should put these comics in a book.

Thank you to James, my agent, for agreeing that these comics should go into a book and for finding Ellen at Icon Books.

Thank you to Ellen at Icon Books for putting these comics into such a lovely book.

And thank you to Rob, for giving these comics a satisfying story arc, and for being the highlight of my life. It's awfully nice of you.

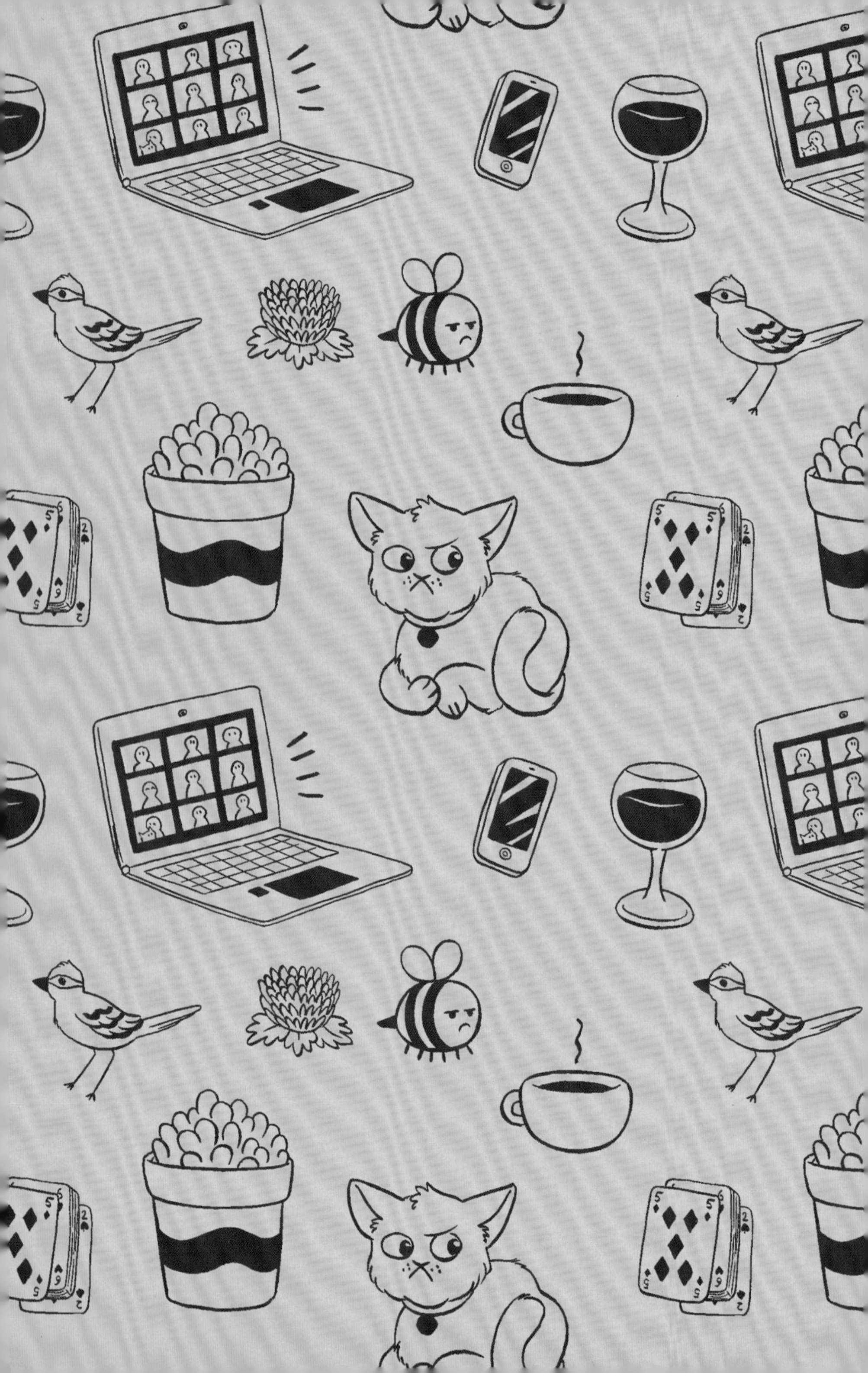